Handbook

2016 Edition

Developed by Royal Rangers®

W9-CHX-472

Gospel Publishing House
Springfield, Missouri
02-0615

For more information about TRaCclub, the online Rangers curriculum source, visit www.RoyalRangers.com.

For Royal Rangers books and supplies, request a Royal Rangers Catalog (order number 75-2028). A Royal Rangers order form listing all Royal Rangers items available may also be requested (order number 75-2003).

Royal Rangers®, the Royal Rangers emblem, and all associated group names and logos are registered trademarks of Gospel Publishing House. Use of these names and logos, as well as the right to establish or conduct a Royal Rangers program, is subject to the terms and conditions defined on the Royal Rangers web site at RoyalRangers.com.

Scripture quotations taken from The Holy Bible, New International Version®, NIV®. Copyright © 1973, 1978, 1984, 2011 by Biblica, Inc.™ Used by permission. All rights reserved worldwide.

The "NIV" and "New International Version" are trademarks registered in the United States Patent and Trademark Offi ce by Biblica, Inc.™

2016 Edition

International Standard Book Number 978-1-60731-259-8

Printed in United States of America

DISCOVERY RANGERS
HANDBOOK

Experience the Journey 6

SECTION ONE
WELCOME TO THE RANGERS EXPERIENCE

1. Welcome to Discovery Rangers! 13
2. The Four Ways We Grow 23
3. A Code to Live By. 27
4. Pledges and Salutes 35
5. You Are Part of Royal Rangers History 41

SECTION TWO
EXPERIENCE THE JOURNEY: THE SEVEN EXPERIENCES OF ROYAL RANGERS

6. The Seven Experiences of Royal Rangers 49
7. Connect with Friends. 57
8. Do Fun Activities 61
9. The Discovery Rangers Advancement Trail 65
10. Special Awards and Insignia 75
11. Learn New Things in Interactive Ways 83
12. Uniforms 87
13. The Patrol System. 93
14. What a Dynamic Patrol Looks Like. 96
15. Leadership Positions and Responsibilities 103

CONTENTS
DISCOVERY RANGER HANDBOOK

16. The Group Leadership Team 119

17. Leading Group Meetings 125

18. Trip Planning 129

19. Patrol of Excellence 133

20. Junior Leadership Development 137

21. Service: It's What Rangers Do 143

SECTION 3
EXPERIENCING TOTAL GROWTH

22. Spiritual Growth: How God Builds a Man 151

23. Physical Growth: How God Builds a Temple 159

24. Continuing the Process: Looking Ahead to
    Adventure Rangers 169

Appendix A: Advancement Logbook 173

Appendix B: Patch and Pin Placement Guide 187

Index 197

*"A man never stands
so tall as when he stoops
to help a boy."*

Johnnie Barnes

Experience the
JOURNEY

Congratulations on being a Discovery Ranger! You are joining an adventure that will be fun, exciting, and full of new experiences. These will help you become the man God has created you to be.

In your Discovery Rangers group, you will have fun! Every week you will get together with friends you already know and make new ones as well. Together you and your friends will have the opportunity to do exciting, new activities that will create stories and memories you will tell over and over again.

Life is an adventure. Adventures are exciting and fun! Discovery Rangers do exactly what their name says— discover! You will have the opportunity to discover and experience exciting, new things. Whether it is skills like First Aid, Rope Craft, or Model Rocketry, or going on a trip where you use the skills you've learned, you will have many opportunities to develop and discover your likes, interests, and just who you are as a young man.

By joining Discovery Rangers, you are part of the larger group called Royal Rangers. As you show up for Discovery Rangers each week, something amazing will happen. While you are doing all those new, exciting things, you will be growing into the man that God has created you to be.

Royal Rangers is fun with a purpose. God has a plan and purpose for your life. Each week you will find out more about God, what His Word says to you, and how you can count on Him to guide and direct you. You will gain confidence by facing the adventures of life with the Rangers who are your friends and the men who are committed to be your leaders and help you be the best you can be.

Well, your adventure is waiting. Grab your handbook and have a blast as you experience the journey!

Karl S. Fleig
Royal Rangers National Director

Royal Rangers PLEDGE

With God's help, I will do my best to serve God, my church, and my fellowman; to live by the Ranger Code; to make the Golden Rule my daily rule.

Royal Rangers EMBLEM

The design of the Royal Rangers Emblem is based on the points of a compass. This is to remind us to direct our attention toward Jesus. The colors of the points have the following meaning:

- The four GOLD points represent the four ways a boy grows: *mentally, physically, spiritually*, and *socially*. (See chapter 2.)

- The four RED points represent the four core beliefs of the Church: *Salvation, Baptism in the Holy Spirit, Divine Healing,* and *the Second Coming*.

- The eight BLUE points represent the eight points of the Royal Rangers Code: *Alert, Clean, Honest, Courageous, Loyal, Courteous, Obedient,* and *Spiritual*.

Note: See pages 30 and 31 for more information on the Royal Rangers Code.

Royal Rangers MOTTO

"Ready"

Meaning of Motto: Ready for anything! Ready to work, play, serve, worship, live, and obey God's Word.

The GOLDEN RULE

"In everything, do to others what you would have them do to you" (Matthew 7:12).

Royal Rangers CODE
A Royal Ranger is . . .

ALERT
He is mentally, physically, and spiritually alert.

CLEAN
He is clean in body, mind, and speech.

HONEST
He does not lie, cheat, or steal.

COURAGEOUS
He is brave in spite of danger, criticism, or threats.

LOYAL
He is faithful to his church, family, outpost, and friends.

COURTEOUS
He is polite, kind, and thoughtful.

OBEDIENT
He obeys his parents, leaders, and those in authority.

SPIRITUAL
He prays, reads the Bible, and witnesses.

Welcome to the
Rangers
Experience

Welcome to Discovery Rangers!

A re you ready for the adventure of a lifetime? If so, you're in the right place. The days ahead will be filled with the greatest adventures of your life. You will experience new things and learn new skills. You will develop new friendships. And you will grow to be like Jesus in a highly relational, fun, and safe place.

"Be strong and very courageous. Be careful to obey all the law . . . do not turn from it to the right or to the left, that you may be successful wherever you go"
(Joshua 1:7).

What Is Discovery Rangers?

Discovery Rangers is a small-group ministry for guys in the third, fourth, and fifth grades. Groups usually hold meetings at the same time every week. These meetings have Bible studies, fun, and special activities called Program Features. Sometimes your group may plan extra events. These could be activities or trips to exciting places.

The advancement system is one of the best parts of Discovery Rangers. This program honors you for your progress. Each step leads you closer to the top goal in Discovery Rangers, the Gold Eagle award.

Many men today will say they earned a merit that gave them the confidence to enter the career they are succeeding in now.

Soaring toward the Gold Eagle

The Trail to the Gold Eagle consists primarily of earning three kinds of merits:

Bible merits give you time to explore God's Word.

Leadership merits will help you to become a good leader.

Skill merits teach skills or special knowledge of subjects, like First Aid Skills, Rope Craft, or Model Rocketry. These are fun and give you time to be with your friends and leaders.

Merits will help you discover new things. Many men today will say they earned a merit that gave them the confidence to enter the career they are succeeding in now. You have more than two hundred merits to choose from. To see a list of the merits you can earn, refer to the advancement logbook section at the back of this book.

Merits Required for the Gold Eagle

EARN AT LEAST 12 OF 15 ORANGE BIBLE MERITS

BIBLE 01 · BIBLE 02 · BIBLE 03 · BIBLE 04 · BIBLE 05

BIBLE 06 · BIBLE 07 · BIBLE 08 · BIBLE 09 · BIBLE 10

BIBLE 11 · BIBLE 12 · BIBLE 13 · BIBLE 14 · BIBLE 15

EARN AT LEAST FOUR (4) RED OR GOLD LEADERSHIP MERITS

LEADERSHIP 101 · LEADERSHIP 102 · LEADERSHIP 103 · LEADERSHIP 104 · LEADERSHIP 105 · LEADERSHIP 106

EARN ALL THREE (3) OF THE REQUIRED BLUE SKILL MERITS

Bible Knowledge   **First Aid Skills**   **Global Missions**

EARN ANY ELEVEN (11) ADDITIONAL BLUE OR GREEN SKILL MERITS

◯ ◯ ◯ ◯ ◯ ◯

◯ ◯ ◯ ◯ ◯

Merits cover a wide range of topics. It usually takes about five weeks to complete a skill merit. When your group finishes one merit, it moves to another.

> Royal Rangers is not just a series of meetings, it's a series of experiences.

Your group chooses the merits you will work on. Some guys love the outdoors. They enjoy camping, fishing, or canoeing. Other adventure seekers may like rock climbing, mountain biking, or skiing. Others may prefer sports like basketball, football, or soccer. And then there's working on cars and building things. Other guys may prefer to explore the latest high-tech gadget or shop at a local electronics store. Still others may want to learn to play an instrument. Those who can play an instrument may want to be in a band with their friends. As you can tell, there is a lot of variety in interests.

Just remember this: Royal Rangers is not just a series of meetings, it's a series of *experiences*. You do fun things and learn new skills. The best experiences are *not* confined to a meeting room. Be creative, make it fun, and make every experience something to remember.

Make every experience something to remember.

Discovery Rangers will lead you through seven unforgettable experiences, known as the Seven Experiences of Royal Rangers.

- CONNECT with friends
- DO fun activities
- GROW in your relationship with God
- LEARN new things in interactive ways
- BELONG to a wholesome community of godly men
- LEAD yourself and influence others
- SERVE others selflessly

Set Your Goals!

You will get out of Discovery Rangers what you put into it. Here are two big goals you can pursue:

- **Earn the Gold Eagle award.** The Gold Eagle represents the highest award you can earn in Discovery Rangers. Boys who earn the Gold Eagle have finished the personal growth and discipleship journey for Discovery Rangers. This award can help you earn the Gold Medal of Achievement (GMA). Details on the Gold Eagle award and the Gold Medal of Achievement can be found in chapter 9.

- **Complete the Junior Leadership Foundations (JLF) training program.** Junior Leadership Foundations is the first step in the junior leader training process in your outpost. More information on Junior Leader Foundations can be found in chapter 20.

Get Ready for an Adventure!

The days ahead of you in Discovery Rangers will be just that, a time of discovery. You'll discover new talents, new skills, and new friends. You will be challenged to grow into the man you were created to be. God created you for a purpose. He has a plan for your life. That plan will lead you into the truest, fullest form of manhood: *Christlike* manhood.

God created mankind, and only God can define what the perfect form of the creation looks like. Jesus Christ was the perfect example of manhood. He was bold. He was caring and compassionate. He was powerful, but He depended on His Father. He created the world, but He became a servant to us all.

He was committed to His purpose, even to the point of enduring a brutal death on a cross. Jesus was a *real man* and a *real servant leader.* By following His example, you can become a real man and a leader of men.

Pursuing Christlike manhood and servant leadership will lead you to true freedom. Discovery Rangers provides what you need to reach this goal. You'll get to connect with other guys your age to form friendships. These friends will support you as you travel God's path for your life. You'll grow by learning new skills and expanding your abilities to lead and serve. You'll also learn to work with other guys to reach common goals. You'll enjoy activities that will enhance your knowledge and skill, while giving you some of the most enjoyable experiences of your life.

Again, welcome to Discovery Rangers. Let the discovery begin!

Discovery Rangers is one of four groups for boys and young men within Royal Rangers.

Ranger Kids: Grades K–2
Discovery Rangers: Grades 3–5
Adventure Rangers: Grades 6–8
Expedition Rangers: Grades 9–12

Each has a group leader and one or more assistant group leaders. The outpost coordinator directs their overall efforts. Together this team is eager to inspire your journey in Royal Rangers.

The Four Ways We Grow

You began growing long before you were born. That growth was easy. Divine programming directed it. But physical development isn't the only way a guy grows. Some kinds of growth require effort on your part. Fortunately, God has provided all you need to grow into the kind of man He wants you to be. As you pursue that goal, the Holy Spirit helps you. He will mold you into true Christlike manhood.

"His divine power has given us everything we need for a godly life through our knowledge of him"
(2 Peter 1:3).

Jesus Was a Boy, Too

In Luke 2:52, the Bible shows Jesus growing into true manhood. Luke describes it this way: "And Jesus grew in wisdom and stature, and in favor with God and man."

From this verse we see that Jesus grew in four important ways:

- **Mentally**—He grew in wisdom
- **Physically**—He grew in stature
- **Spiritually**—He grew in favor with God
- **Socially**—He grew in favor with men

Christlike manhood requires balanced growth in all four areas. Discovery Rangers challenges you to grow these ways:

Mentally—Skill-building activities promote growth in all four areas. But mental growth is the main target.

Physically—Rigorous physical activity causes your body to grow. This activity may be related to skills you learn. Or, it may be a regular part of the meetings you attend. To be strong and healthy, you need good health habits. These include proper eating, rest, and exercise.

Spiritually—Bible merits and weekly devotions promote spiritual growth.

Socially—You will learn leadership, teamwork, and social skills. These skills are learned as you earn leadership merits and as you fill leadership roles in your group.

The challenge may be difficult. It may take a long time. You may not always understand the process God takes you through as you grow into manhood. But you can trust that God is in control. He will grow you into His image and He will not leave the job unfinished.

"He who began a good work in you will carry it on to completion until the day of Christ Jesus" (Philippians 1:6).

A Code to Live By

Every guy dreams of becoming a man. But when do you become a man? Does it happen when you grow facial hair? When your voice gets deep? When you learn to drive? When you can vote? When you turn twenty-one? Or is there more to becoming a man than physical development, age, or skills? Of course there is! To be a real man, you have to be like Jesus.

How to Become a Man

The measure of a man is found in his maturity. If you are mature, you are responsible for yourself. You serve others. You keep your word. You do what you're supposed to do. You don't have to be bigger, stronger, or older. You can be mature right now.

By now you should be responsible for these things:

√ Brushing your teeth

√ Dressing yourself

√ Making your bed

√ Picking up after yourself

√ Saying please and thank you

√ Guarding your words to avoid hurting others

√ Helping others

As you take on more responsibility, you become more mature.

It may be cute to watch a one-year-old toss and leave his toys on the floor, but when a ten-year-old does that, we call it immaturity. When a young man is responsible, he gains the respect of his peers and most adults.

The apostle Paul urged Titus, a young church leader, to "encourage the young men to be self-controlled" (Titus 2:6). In other words, to be mature. On the journey to maturity, you'll accept responsibility for yourself and for others by serving them.

Jesus Is Our Example

Jesus is the perfect example of what it means to be a man. He was fully God and fully man. He was tempted just like you are. Think about that! Every temptation you've faced, Jesus faced.

Yet He never gave in to it! He accepted responsibility for himself—for His actions and for the development of His character.

You are at the trailhead of your manhood, the start. Like any journey, it begins by choosing your path.

The Choice Is Your Responsibility

You are at the trailhead of your manhood, the start. Like any journey, it begins by choosing your path. Unfortunately, many guys take the wrong path. The Bible says we are all like sheep who have gone astray; we have lived life our own way (Isaiah 53:6). But the result of living life our own way is very sad and very predictable. It leads to loss, to death, and to separation from God and those we love (Romans 6:23). The better path is to follow Christ. It is the only path to becoming a real man. Choosing this path leads to a full life that money, popularity, and admiration can never buy. It leads to the greatest gift—the gift of real life, never-ending life. You only get that by following Jesus (Romans 6:23).

So every day you have a choice to make. Who will you follow?

- Yourself, which leads to death
- Jesus, who leads to life

This is a choice only you can make. It is your responsibility. Your choice has consequences. Following yourself will lead to immaturity, loss, and death. Following Jesus will lead to mature manhood, fulfillment, and life. Choose Jesus!

A Code to Live By

Being a Royal Ranger is about being a fully alive guy, being a committed follower of Christ, and being like Jesus. The Royal Rangers Code describes the character of Jesus. As you read the Bible and learn more about God, you will see that these qualities describe Him well. Memorize these. Live the Code. Be like Jesus.

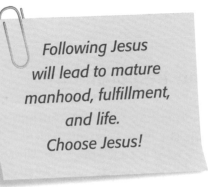

Following Jesus will lead to mature manhood, fulfillment, and life. Choose Jesus!

Royal Rangers CODE

A Royal Ranger is . . .

ALERT He is mentally, physically, and spiritually alert.	"Train yourself to be godly. For physical training is of some value, but godliness has value for all things, holding promise for both the present life and the life to come" (1 Timothy 4:7,8).
CLEAN He is clean in body, mind, and speech.	"Don't let anyone look down on you because you are young, but set an example for the believers in speech, in conduct, in love, in faith and in purity" (1 Timothy 4:12).
HONEST He does not lie, cheat, or steal.	"Whoever walks in integrity walks securely, but whoever takes crooked paths will be found out" (Proverbs 10:9). "Each of you must put off falsehood and speak truthfully to your neighbor, for we are all members of one body" (Ephesians 4:25).
COURAGEOUS He is brave in spite of danger, criticism, or threats.	"When they saw the courage of Peter and John and realized that they were unschooled, ordinary men, they were astonished and they took note that these men had been with Jesus" (Acts 4:13).
LOYAL He is faithful to his church, family, outpost, and friends.	"After David had finished talking with Saul, Jonathan became one in spirit with David, and he loved him as himself" (1 Samuel 18:1).
COURTEOUS He is polite, kind, and thoughtful.	"Do nothing out of selfish ambition or vain conceit. Rather, in humility value others above yourselves" (Philippians 2:3).
OBEDIENT He obeys his parents, leaders, and those in authority.	"Fear God and keep his commandments, for this is the duty of all mankind" (Eccleiastes 12:13).
SPIRITUAL He prays, reads the Bible, and witnesses.	"He answered, 'Love the Lord your God with all your heart and with all your soul and with all your strength and with all your mind'; and, 'Love your neighbor as yourself'" (Luke 10:27).

As you become better friends with Jesus, you will gain strength. Others will admire your strength and want it. Your example will give you influence in their lives. By following Jesus, you will gain the ability to lead others to Christ. And then you won't be the only Christian at school and elsewhere. You'll be surrounded by boys who share your goal—to be like Jesus, to have a personal relationship with Him, and to be real men. Together, you'll influence everyone around you!

The Royal Rangers Pledge, the Royal Rangers Motto, and the Golden Rule remind you to serve others the way Jesus did. The Bible says Jesus didn't leave heaven so others could serve Him. He came to earth to serve (Mark 10:45). We should do the same. The Code tells us to be like Jesus. The Pledge, Motto, and Golden Rule remind us who to serve. That's how you become a real man—become alive in your relationship with Jesus and serve others.

So when do you become a man? Each time you choose to follow Jesus' example in character and service to others you mature. When done over time, that consistent choice builds you into an extraordinary man who influences everyone around you. That's how you accept responsibility for yourself and for others.

If you have not already done so, make the choice: follow Jesus. Be a Christlike man and a lifelong servant leader! Make that decision today and every day.

Pledges and Salutes

As part of the Opening Ceremony for weekly outpost meetings, many groups recite the pledges to the United States and Christian flags and recite the Royal Rangers Pledge. This chapter gives you the words to say and the ways to salute.

Some groups also choose to have all their members stand in an organized formation. Some may also choose to use a color guard to present the flags in a more formal setting. Information on formations, ceremonies, and color guards can be found online at RoyalRangers.com.

Pledge of Allegiance to the United States Flag

Salute by placing your right hand over your heart.

"I pledge allegiance to the Flag of the United States of America and to the Republic for which it stands, one Nation under God, indivisible, with liberty and justice for all."

Pledge to the Christian Flag

Salute by placing your right hand over your heart.

"I pledge allegiance to the Christian flag and to the Savior for whose Kingdom it stands, one brotherhood, uniting all true Christians in service and in love."

Pledge to the Bible

Salute by holding both hands out in front of you, together, flat, with palms facing up, as if holding a Bible.

"I pledge allegiance to the Bible, God's Holy Word. I will make it a lamp unto my feet, and a light unto my path, and will hide its words in my heart that I might not sin against God."

Royal Rangers Pledge

Recite the pledge after raising your right hand, with upper arm horizontal to the ground and forearm pointing up, your elbow forming a right angle, hand open and flat with palm facing forward.

"With God's help, I will do my best to serve God, my church, and my fellowman; to live by the Ranger Code; to make the Golden Rule my daily rule."

Displaying the Flags

On a flag pole

Always treat the United States flag with the highest respect. You may fly the flag continuously, both day and night. However, the flag must be visible at night. It must be lit up either by a streetlight or another light source.

No flag may fly above the United States flag on the same mast; however, other flags may fly below the United States flag on the same line or mast.

As you raise the flag on a pole or mast, the flag should be unfolded and held out by a second person while you pull the line upward. You should raise the flag quickly, but lower it slowly, with dignity. The United States flag must be higher than all other flags.

The Christian flag is flown at the same height as other non-national flags, such as those of states.

The United States flag is to be flown at half-mast while mourning the death of a person and on Memorial Day (until noon). When hoisting the flag, raise it to the top of the mast first and then lower it halfway. When lowering the flag, raise the flag to the top first, then lower and remove it from the mast.

On a platform

If the flag is on the platform, the United States flag should be on the audience's left, with all other flags to the audience's right. If United States flag is hung on the wall, it should be placed behind the speaker with the stars in the upper left corner of the flag.

When the United States flag is displayed in a group of other flags, it should be at the center or at the highest point. Again, it can be at the audience's left.

In a procession

When carried in a procession with other flags, the United States flag should be either on the right of the line of marchers holding the flags or in the center in front of the other flags.

During the ceremony of hoisting or lowering the United States flag, or when the flag is passing in a parade or in a review, those in view of the flag should come to attention and face the flag. In uniform or out you should place your right hand over your heart. If a man or boy has on a hat that is not a part of his uniform, he should remove it with his right hand and place it over his heart. Women may keep their hats on.

Caring for the Flag

The United States flag may be mended or dry-cleaned. When the flag is soiled or torn beyond repair, it may be destroyed by burning or burial during a special ceremony for the occasion.

When not being flown or displayed, the flag should be folded neatly so that the top and bottom attachment grommets are easily reached.

How To Fold the Flag   Folded Flag

You Are Part of Royal Rangers History

One of the best things about being a boy is you have lots of dreams. Your Rangers leaders want to help you make those dreams come true. Rangers will help you go far. When you are a Royal Ranger, you are building on more than fifty years of history. You stand on the shoulders of others who have done big things.

Rangers have become successful businessmen and humanitarians, as well as community and political leaders. Many have also gone on to become pastors, missionaries, evangelists, architects, accountants, lawyers, tradesmen, sports celebrities, musicians, military personnel, and more. What they all have in common is they are Royal Rangers. Once a Ranger, always a Ranger!

You can experience the same things they did, learn from them, stand on their shoulders, reach higher, and go farther than they did. The power of history is that you can benefit from the successes of those who have gone before you. Go far so others can benefit from your life, too. Here's our past; start your future!

ROYAL RANGERS HISTORY

1962—Royal Rangers started under the direction of Rev. Johnnie Barnes, district youth director from North Texas, as a ministry designed to disciple young men and keep them in our churches.

1963—The Leadership Training Course (LTC) is created to train leaders to disciple future men.

1964—The first districtwide summer camps were held.

1964—The Gold Medal of Achievement and Medal of Valor awards are first offered.

1966—Royal Rangers ministries are established in Latin America and Asia.

1966—The Frontiersmen Camping Fellowship (FCF) is formed.

1968—The first National Training Camps (NTC) are held.

1972—The first national event, a National FCF Rendezvous, was held near Springfield, Missouri.

1974—The first National Camporama was held at the Air Force Academy in Colorado Springs, Colorado.

1978—The second National Camporama was held in Farragut, Idaho.

1982—The third National Camporama was held in Pigeon Forge, Tennessee.

1986—The National Royal Rangers Center, also known as Camp Eagle Rock, near Eagle Rock, Missouri, was dedicated. The fourth National Camporama is held there.

1989—Johnnie Barnes, who led Royal Rangers from its inception, passes away. He led Royal Rangers for twenty-seven years, leaving an extensive legacy and thousands of men and boys who are serving Jesus Christ.

1989—Rev. Ken Hunt becomes the second national Royal Rangers commander.

1990—The fifth National Camporama is held at Camp Eagle Rock.

1994—The sixth National Camporama takes place at Camp Eagle Rock.

1998—The seventh National Camporama is held at Camp Eagle Rock.

1999—Rev. Richard Mariott becomes the third national Royal Rangers commander.

2002—Royal Rangers International (RRI) is formed to help coordinate the efforts and needs of the approximately forty-five countries using Royal Rangers at the time.

2002—The eighth National Camporama takes place at Camp Eagle Rock.

2006—The ninth National Camporama is held at Camp Eagle Rock.

2007—Rev. Doug Marsh becomes the fourth national Royal Rangers commander.

2012—The tenth National Camporama and fiftieth anniversary celebration takes place at Camp Eagle Rock.

2014—Rev. Karl Fleig becomes the fifth national Royal Rangers commander.

2016—The eleventh National Camporama is held at Camp Eagle Rock.

These men are part of Royal Rangers history as well. They were Royal Rangers as boys, just like you.

Hal Donaldson, Royal Ranger & Humanitarian

Hal Donaldson serves as president and CEO of Convoy of Hope, a disaster relief organization that provides food, medical help, and other services to people worldwide.

Doug Clay, Royal Ranger & Minister

Doug Clay serves as the general treasurer of the General Council of the Assemblies of God, the national organization for all Assemblies of God churches.

Mark Broberg, Royal Ranger & Missionary

Mark Broberg serves as an Assemblies of God world missionary to the people of Russia.

Experience the Journey:

The Seven Experiences of Royal Rangers

The Seven Experiences of Royal Rangers

In the days ahead, you will face new things. Your character will decide how you react to each challenge. The standards and values you set now will define your character. They will rule your actions and reactions.

It is essential that you base your standards on a code of conduct that is not subject to change. The code you pick should be universal, and eternal. The Word of God is such a code. You can use it to guide your actions throughout your daily journey.

Seven experiences will shape your character. These are the building blocks of Royal Rangers.

As a Royal Ranger, you will CONNECT with friends.

"By this everyone will know that you are my disciples, if you love one another" **(John 13:35).**

When it comes to having a great time, what you're doing is less crucial than who you're with. Spending a day at a theme park riding rides alone doesn't sound fun, does it? But friends change things. In Rangers, you will make friends who love God.

As you participate in fun activities, you will make friends. Picture yourself in Rangers. You could be playing flag football. Or, you could be fishing a quiet stream (and later bragging about your catch, of course), or pulling together a garage band. Group activities will help you will strengthen existing friendships and find new ones. (See chapter 7.)

As a Royal Ranger, you will DO fun activities.

"Whatever your hand finds to do, do it with all your might" (Ecclesiastes 9:10).

Doing things is a core part of Royal Rangers. Doing activities will help you learn new skills or sharpen old ones. Your mind and body will grow, too. You will engage mentally in the process of learning new skills. Some activities will force you to use your body. If you're going to hike a trail, or play football with your friends, you're going to use your body. You'll engage spiritually by applying spiritual truths to your life. You'll also engage socially as you take part in the process with others. (See chapter 8.)

As a Royal Ranger, you will GROW in your relationship with God.

"Value others above yourselves, not looking to your own interests but each of you to the interests of the others" (Philippians 2:3,4).

Life is growth. Without growth, death comes. That's just a rule of nature. Royal Rangers will help you grow in your relationship with God on three trails of achievement.

Advancement Trail

In Rangers you explore new interests and develop new skills! And as you progress, you will be recognized for your accomplishments. (See chapter 9.)

Leadership

Do you know you're already influencing people around you every day? In Rangers we learn servant leadership by completing leadership merits, attending Junior Leadership Foundations, completing junior leadership development camps, and by practicing good leadership in your weekly meetings and regular outings. (See chapter 13.)

Service

Jesus is the ultimate servant. He humbled himself. Even though He is God, He came to earth. He did that to help us recover our lost relationship with Him. You, too, will be given the opportunity to serve others in Royal Rangers: by participating in service and outreach projects, by giving to missions, and much more. Special awards are available to recognize individuals for their service. Service projects are also a part of all leadership merits (See chapter 21.)

As a Royal Ranger, you will LEARN new things in interactive ways.

"And the things you have heard me say in the presence of many witnesses entrust to reliable people who will also be qualified to teach others" (2 Timothy 2:2).

Rangers is fun, interactive, hands-on learning. You will hear, see, do, and teach:

- **Hear.** Someone gives you new information or reviews stuff you already know. This can be given out loud, by reading something in print or online, or by watching a movie clip, human video, or skit. This is one way we pick up information.

- **See.** This involves a demonstration, a chart, a picture or a video, something that illustrates or represents what you're learning in a visual way. Sometimes we hear and see something at the same time.

- **Do.** For most guys, the best way to learn how to do something is to actually do it hands-on. This is where we practice what we have heard and seen demonstrated.

- **Teach.** Finally, we can seal what we are learning by telling someone else what we have learned. Teaching others strengthens your knowledge and helps others.

Learning is growing, and growing is living. You will have more success as you learn, discover, and develop your God-given talents. (See chapter 11.)

As a Royal Ranger, you will BELONG to a wholesome community of godly men.

> "If we walk in the light, as he is in the light, we have fellowship with one another, and the blood of Jesus, his Son, purifies us from all sin" (1 John 1:7).

You are a vital part of the body of men in your church. Men need support, friendship, and testing. Those things are a natural part of spending time with other men. This group gives you the chance to impact other men within the group and to join together for a common cause.

Wearing a uniform is an easy way you can let others know that you're a Royal Ranger. Lots of Rangers gear is available to build a sense of belonging. (See chapter 12.)

As a Royal Ranger, you will LEAD yourself and influence others.

> "And David shepherded them with integrity of heart; with skillful hands he led them" (Psalm 78:72).

Leadership is a core part of Royal Rangers. You'll start learning how to be a leader in Junior Leadership Foundations with an introduction to leadership interview. You'll continue learning by earning leadership merits and completing district leadership development camps. You will be involved in leadership at every turn in Royal Rangers. You'll even learn about leadership during your weekly meetings as you serve your group in various roles. (See chapter 17.)

As a Royal Ranger, you will SERVE others selflessly.

> "For the Son of Man did not come to be served, but to serve, and to give his life as a ransom for many" (Mark 10:45).

Service and ministry projects are common in Royal Rangers. Jesus served everyone around Him sacrificially, so we do the same. (See chapter 21.)

As you enjoy Discovery Rangers, let these seven experiences shape you. God wants you to be like Jesus. He is our model of manhood and servant leadership. Allow these experiences to impact you and you will become more like Jesus. As that happens, you will become the man God designed you to be.

Connect with Friends

One of the great benefits of being a Royal Ranger is connecting with other guys. You'll get to have good, clean fun with your group. You'll create great memories. And you'll establish lasting Christ-centered friendships.

Making friends is not hard, but it does take some time, commitment, and patience since your friend probably isn't perfect.

Here's What You Need to Do

Get Involved: To make and keep friends, do things other people do. You can't form friendships sitting alone at home. So get involved, get active, and stick with it.

Find Common Interests: In order to have a friend, you have to be a friend. Everyone has things they like to do. As you look for new friends, look for people who share some of the same wholesome interests as you. When you find things you have in common, enjoy those things together.

Spend Time Together: Friendships take time to develop, and becoming close friends takes awhile. But the best way to become good friends is to do fun things together.

Be Considerate: Think about how what you do affects others. Everyone likes being with people who are caring and encouraging. Few people want to be around those who are selfish and rude. Put the interests of others ahead of your own. Then, you will be someone everyone wants to be around.

Learn to Forgive: Forgiveness is a big part of any relationship. None of us is perfect. If you and another guy are friends long enough, one of you will make the other mad. That's the way it is. But true friends are willing to overlook each other's faults and mistakes. They forgive each other, and they forgive themselves. And sometimes that's the hardest part.

Royal Rangers is a great way to make friends. You and your fellow Rangers will have lots of great fun together. Activities like basketball games and water fights will help you develop new friendships and strengthen old ones. Activities will also draw other guys to your group, your church, and ultimately to Jesus.

Be a friend to everyone in your group. Make guys who visit feel welcome. Be friendly and kind. And be quick to involve visitors in your activities.

HOW CAN YOU LEAD OTHERS TO JESUS?

You can help someone become a Christian by having him follow these three simple steps, called "The ABCs of Salvation."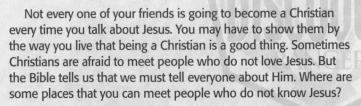

1. Admit that he has sinned (done things that are wrong).
2. Believe in Jesus.
3. Confess and turn away from sin (try not to do things that are wrong).

Not every one of your friends is going to become a Christian every time you talk about Jesus. You may have to show them by the way you live that being a Christian is a good thing. Sometimes Christians are afraid to meet people who do not love Jesus. But the Bible tells us that we must tell everyone about Him. Where are some places that you can meet people who do not know Jesus?

- At school
- At sporting events
- At clubs and special interest groups
- At places where you volunteer to help

Be prepared to answer some simple questions:

- Who is Jesus? *He is the Son of God. He has the power to forgive us for everything we've done wrong.*
- What is Jesus like? *He is a friend. He loves us. He wants to help us. He wants us all to go to heaven.*
- What does Jesus want from us? *He wants us to love Him. He wants us to know that our sins are forgiven. He wants us to love and help others.*

When a friend has accepted Jesus, you can help him in different ways. You can invite him to church, pray for him, talk with him, and introduce him to leaders who can help him. Pray and ask Jesus to bring people into your life that you can witness to. Then be alert and ready by behaving as a Christian should at all times.

Do Fun Activities

Discovery Rangers will keep you active. And you will get to do some fun group activities.

These activities are often tied to merits. You can earn more than two hundred skill merits. You can also learn to be a leader. Leadership merits have lots of activities. These activities will help your group learn the skills needed to work as a team. And you will help your church or community.

Variety Is Fun!

Royal Rangers has a lot of group activities. You will be able to try new things and learn new skills. Maybe you will even develop some new interests.

Most of your activities will fit into one of five groups. A good program draws activities from each group as often as possible.

- **Outdoor activities:** Having fun outdoors has always been a major part of Royal Rangers. And it still is. Today there are still lots of fun things to do outdoors.

- **Sports**: Sports are popular with guys of all ages.

- **Trade skills:** In the future you will have many job options. However, you must be properly prepared. Many of the things you learn through skill merits can serve as the basis for a life's work.

- **Technology:** You use more high-tech tools and toys than guys in the past. This knowledge can be a great asset and a source of great fun and learning.

- **Arts and ministry:** God expects all His people to share the gospel and help others. Arts and ministry merits can help you find your own gifts and abilities.

Refer to the advancement logbook in the back of this handbook for a list of available merits.

District and National Events

Your district hosts lots of great activities. These may include summer camps, Ranger Derbies, sports days, or chances to develop as a junior leader. Check with your district for details.

National events occur less often. But when they do happen, they are tons of fun. In fact, national events are so much fun that they

are not likely to be forgotten. Many guys have only one or two chances to attend some events. One of those is National Camporama. It's the best event ever! You won't want to miss it.

Another great event is the National Rendezvous. It's an event for members of the Frontiersmen Camping Fellowship. You may know Frontiersmen Camping Fellowship as FCF. Rendezvous is full of competition, activities, and, most importantly, lots of great times. FCF and Rendezvous are for guys in Adventure Rangers and Expedition Rangers and adult leaders.

Camporama and Rendezvous are two separate events. Each event is held every four years. The events take place at Eagle Rock, Missouri. That is where the national Royal Rangers campground is. Visit RoyalRangers.com for details. (Always ask your parents before going online.)

You Make All the Difference

You play a key role in the success of your group's activities. You can help make an event a great time for everyone. You do this by using your skills and abilities to help plan and lead events. If you invite your friends and encourage others, you will help get people excited.

The Discovery Rangers Advancement Trail

Get ready for a great adventure! The Discovery Rangers Advancement Trail is filled with great opportunities. You will get to have fun, grow, and develop new skills. And you can be sure the Advancement Trail will be full of friends and adventure.

Overview

The Advancement Trail has fifteen steps. Steps must be completed in order beginning with the White Falcon. Each step requires you to do a certain number and type of merits. As you complete each step you will get an award such as a medal, patch, ribbon, neck medallion, or certificate.

Your goal should be to complete the entire Trail before you move to Adventure Rangers. That will push you, but you can make it. To stay on track, you will need to finish one advancement step every three months, but you can move more quickly if you like.

Walk the Advancement Trail with a friend. That way you can keep each other on track! As you travel the Trail, you'll pick up some great memories.

Merits

Merits are awards. They are earned by completing a set of fun and interactive requirements related to a topic. Merits are classified by type and by color. Merit colors refer to the color of border used on the merit patch, and they generally correspond with a specific age group. The following table identifies the types and colors of merits for each age group.

TYPE	DISCOVERY RANGERS	ADVENTURE RANGERS	EXPEDITION RANGERS
Bible	Orange	Brown	Spirit Challenges
Leadership	Red	Gold	Sky Blue
Skill	Blue	Green	Silver

- *Bible merits* help you to grow as a Christlike man. God's Word talks a lot about issues you face. God can help you live well. Discovery Rangers Bible merits have an orange border. They are earned by completing eight Bible lessons. (Note: All eight Bible lessons may be from the orange Bible lesson category. Or, one or two lessons may be special things approved by your leader. He can approve things like Bible studies created by your church leaders, district kids camp, and similar activities).

- *Leadership merits* sharpen your ability to impact your world and serve others. Your group leader will teach these during the regular meetings. Or he may teach them on a fun weekend outing. Discovery Rangers leadership merits are red. These merits are recommended to be taught twice a year. More information on leadership merits can be found in chapter 20, Junior Leadership Development.

- *Skill merits* push you to learn new skills and to apply skills you have mastered. These merits focus on activities you will like, and can be earned with your group, friends, parents, and even on your own. A list of all available skill merits is at RoyalRangers.com. (Check with a parent before going online.)

Advancement Steps

The merits you earn form the building blocks of the advancement system. They allow you to earn special recognition each quarter and each year. The following tables show the requirements for each sequential advancement step.

New Member Requirements

As a new Discovery Ranger, you must complete the following requirements before earning the White Falcon award.

- Be a boy in the third, fourth, or fifth grade.

- Complete your outpost's requirements for new members, if any.

- Recite from memory the Royal Rangers Pledge, Code, Motto, the meaning of the points of the Emblem, and the Golden Rule. (See pages 8 and 9.)

- Review the booklet *Preventing Child and Substance Abuse*. Talk about what you read with your parents or legal guardians. This booklet can be found online at RoyalRangers.com.

- Attend three regular Discovery Rangers meetings.

Year 1 - Trail to the Gold Falcon

ADVANCEMENT STEP	BIBLE MERITS (ORANGE)		SKILL MERITS ELECTIVE (BLUE OR GREEN)		SKILL MERITS REQUIRED[1] (BLUE)		LEADERSHIP MERITS (RED OR GOLD)	
	EARN	TOTAL	EARN	TOTAL	EARN	TOTAL	EARN	TOTAL
White Falcon	1	1	1	1	-	-	-	-
Red Falcon	1	2	1	2	-	-	-	-
Bronze Falcon	1	3	1	3	-	-	-	-
Silver Falcon	1	4	1	4	1*	1	1*	1
Gold Falcon[2]	-	4	-	4	-	1	-	1

*These merits may be earned at any point prior to completing the Silver Falcon award.

Additional requirement for the Gold Falcon award:

- Recite again from memory the Royal Rangers Pledge, Code, Motto, the meaning of the points of the Emblem, and the Golden Rule.

[1]See note 1 on page 70.
[2]See note 2 on page 70.

Year 2 - Trail to the Gold Hawk

ADVANCEMENT STEP	BIBLE MERITS (ORANGE)		SKILL MERITS ELECTIVE (BLUE OR GREEN)		SKILL MERITS REQUIRED[1] (BLUE)		LEADERSHIP MERITS (RED OR GOLD)	
	EARN	TOTAL	EARN	TOTAL	EARN	TOTAL	EARN	TOTAL
White Hawk	1	5	1	5	-	1	-	1
Red Hawk	1	6	1	6	-	1	-	1
Bronze Hawk	1	7	1	7	-	1	-	1
Silver Hawk	1	8	1	8	1*	2	1*	2
Gold Hawk[2]	-	8	-	8	-	2	-	2

*These merits may be earned at any point prior to completing the Silver Hawk award.

Additional requirements for the Gold Hawk award:

- Recite again from memory the Royal Rangers Pledge, Code, Motto, the meaning of the points of the Emblem, and the Golden Rule.

- Be a Gold Falcon award recipient at least six months, or be a graduate of third grade.

- Serve in one or more leadership positions in Discovery Rangers for at least six months.

- Show your ability to present the plan of salvation to someone. (See chapter 7.)

[1]See note 1 on page 70.
[2]See note 2 on page 70.

Year 3 - Trail to the Gold Eagle

ADVANCEMENT STEP	BIBLE MERITS (ORANGE)		SKILL MERITS ELECTIVE (BLUE OR GREEN)		SKILL MERITS REQUIRED[1] (BLUE)		LEADERSHIP MERITS (RED OR GOLD)	
	EARN	TOTAL	EARN	TOTAL	EARN	TOTAL	EARN	TOTAL
White Eagle	1	9	1	9	-	2	-	2
Red Eagle	1	10	1	10	-	2	-	2
Bronze Eagle	1	11	1	11	-	2	-	2
Silver Eagle	1	12	-	11	1*	3	2*	4
Gold Eagle[2]	-	12	-	11	-	3	-	4

*These merits may be earned at any point prior to completing the Silver Eagle award.

Additional requirements for the Gold Eagle award:

- Recite again from memory the Royal Rangers Pledge, Code, Motto, the meaning of the points of the Emblem, and the Golden Rule.

- Be a Gold Hawk award recipient for no less than nine months, or be a graduate of the fourth grade.

- Serve in one or more leadership positions in Discovery Rangers for an additional six months, for a total of twelve months.

- Show your ability to present the plan of salvation to someone. (See chapter 7.)

[1]One of the following required skill merits must be earned for each of the Gold Falcon, Gold Hawk, and Gold Eagle awards: blue Bible skill merit, blue Global Missions skill merit, and blue First Aid Skills skill merit.

[2]An application must be submitted to the national Royal Rangers office to receive the Gold Falcon, Gold Hawk, or Gold Eagle awards.

Bronze Buffaloes

Bronze Buffalo awards are available to Discovery Rangers who have earned the Gold Eagle award and want to continue advancement in Discovery Rangers. The award insignia is a bronze buffalo pin you wear on the cloth portion of your Gold Eagle award medal. The insignia can also be a bronze star you wear on the Gold Eagle award ribbon. You may earn and wear up to two Bronze Buffaloes.

For each Bronze Buffalo award, you must meet the following requirements:

- Earn one additional red leadership merit

- Earn two additional blue skill merits

- Earn one additional orange Bible merit

Advancement Restrictions

Although the advancement system allows a lot of flexibility and personal choice, you need to know there are some limitations:

- All Discovery Rangers advancement requirements must be met before you graduate from the eighth grade.

- You may earn any color merit, but as a Discovery Ranger you may only earn advancement steps for Discovery Rangers and Ranger Kids. This allows you to complete any unfinished advancement work from Ranger Kids.

- A merit can only be counted once to satisfy advancement requirements. Merits applied to your Discovery Rangers advancement steps, for instance, cannot be counted again in Adventure Rangers.

Gold Medal of Achievement

The Gold Medal of Achievement (GMA) is a special Royal Rangers award that provides recognition to boys who have demonstrated exceptional achievement in the program. This prestigious award can only be achieved after many years of continuous effort. To earn the GMA you must meet the following requirements:

- Earn the highest award in any TWO of the following groups:

  ◊ Discovery Rangers—Gold Eagle

  ◊ Adventure Rangers—Adventure Gold Award

  ◊ Expedition Rangers—E3 Award

- Read the entire Bible or listen to it as an audio book.

- Be at least twelve years old.

- Be an active member of a Royal Rangers outpost for at least five years.

- Complete the GMA Capstone Project. (See RoyalRangers.com.)

All requirements for the GMA must be met before you reach your eighteenth birthday.

Special Honors with the GMA

Boys who earn the highest award in any three age groups, including Ranger Kids, will receive the additional recognition of the GMA *with Merit*. Boys who earn the highest award in all four age groups will receive the GMA *with Honors*.

Requirements for the GMA with Merit:

- Meet all requirements for the GMA.
- Earn the highest award in any THREE age groups:
  ◊ Ranger Kids—Gold Trail Award
  ◊ Discovery Rangers—Gold Eagle Award
  ◊ Adventure Rangers—Adventure Gold Award
  ◊ Expedition Rangers—E3 Award

Requirements for the GMA with Honors:

- Meet all requirements for the GMA.
- Earn the highest award in all FOUR age groups:
  ◊ Ranger Kids—Gold Trail Award
  ◊ Discovery Rangers—Gold Eagle Award
  ◊ Adventure Rangers—Adventure Gold Award
  ◊ Expedition Rangers—E3 Award

VALOR

SERVICE

COURAGE

MERIT

SERVICE

Firearm Safety

has fulfilled the requirements of the Firearm Safety Merit and is hereby granted the privilege of carrying and using a BB gun or air rifle during Royal Rangers sponsored events.

COMMANDER

THE THREE LAWS

OOL USE

Tool Craft Safety

has fulfilled the requirements of the Tool Craft Merit and is hereby granted the privilege of carrying and using outdoor tools.

COMMANDER

Special Awards and Insignia

You can be honored for more than just your work on the Advancement Trail. You can also earn special awards. These awards honor great successes or something special you've done for Rangers. You must meet certain guidelines to earn each of these awards.

Your local leaders can approve some of the awards. However, some awards require district or national approval. You can find applications for the awards that need special approval at RoyalRangers.com. Requirements for each award can be found on the application.

Medal of Valor

The Medal of Valor is the highest award a boy or leader can receive in Royal Rangers. You earn this award if you risk your life while saving someone else's life. The national office decides who gets the award.

Medal of Courage

The Medal of Courage is similar to the Medal of Valor. It is presented a boy or a leader who saves the life of another person. It does not require the rescuer's own life be at risk. The national office decides who gets the award.

National Medal of Merit

The national office gives the National Medal of Merit to boys or adult leaders. Those who get the medal have shown excellent service and devotion to the national program. The national office decides who gets the award.

National Outstanding Service Award

The national office gives the National Outstanding Service Award to boys or leaders who have given outstanding service to the national program. The national office decides who gets the award.

Missions Project Award

Your local leaders can give you this award. To be eligible, you must take part in a denominationally approved home or international missions project. The project must last at least five days. Travel time is not counted toward the five days.

District Medal of Merit

Your district leader can give you this award. It is given to Rangers who have shown very good service and dedication to the district program. District leaders decide who gets the medal.

District Outstanding Service Award

Your district leader can give you this award. The award is given to Rangers who have given very good service to the district program. District directors decide who gets these awards.

Mile Awards

Mile Awards provide recognition to boys or leaders who have participated in a twenty-five-, fifty-, or one-hundred-mile hike, canoe trip, or bike trip. This may include backpacking, kayaking, rafting, or something similar. You may not use any form of motorized transportation. The miles counted may be completed over multiple consecutive days. However, you may not accumulate miles from separate events. Award patches may be worn on the awards vest in the same location as regular activity patches. Multiple patches may not be earned from the same event.

Mile awards are a big triumph and require a lot of effort to achieve. You should see a doctor and get proper physical training before attempting a long-distance event.

You do not have to apply for Mile Awards. Your leader presents Mile Awards after you earn them.

Tool Craft Safety Card

When you earn your Tool Craft merit, you qualify for the Tool Craft Safety Card. This card shows that you have learned the principles of safe tool handling and have shown that you can use camp tools safely and effectively. This card should be carried with you during all Royal Rangers camping events.

Firearm Safety Card

If you have earned the Firearm Safety merit, you qualify for the Firearm Safety Card. This shows you have completed the safety course required to use air rifles and firearms. This card may be required to participate in Royal Rangers shooting events.

Special Awards Index

The following table shows the level at which each special award is approved. It also shows which awards are available to leaders, boys, or both. Awards requiring national approval must be requested by using an award application. The application can be downloaded at RoyalRangers.com. Contact your district for application procedures for awards requiring district approval. No applications are required for awards requiring local approval.

AWARD	LOCAL	DISTRICT	NATIONAL
Medal of Valor			L / DR
Medal of Courage			L / DR
National Medal of Merit			L / DR
National Outstanding Service Award			L / DR
Missions Project Award	L / DR		
District Medal of Merit		L / DR	
District Outstanding Service Award		L / DR	
Mile Awards	L / DR		
Tool Craft Safety Card	L / DR		
Firearm Safety Card	L / DR		

L = Award may be earned by adult leaders.
DR = Award may be earned by Discovery Rangers.

"The greatest reward for a man's toil is not what he gets for it, but what he becomes by it."

John Ruskin

Learn New Things in Interactive Ways

The best way for most people to learn a new skill is by using the "hear, see, do, teach" method. This method of learning uses all the ways we learn. The process is an easy one to follow. And it makes learning fun and beneficial.

Hear: The first step is to hear the new information. This could be a simple step-by-step account of a process. It could also be the reasons a skill is valuable, or how the skill might be used.

See: Next is demonstration. You need to see how something is done. This could include pictures, charts, maps, and physical objects. It could be anything that helps you get a real sense of the subject. Sometimes you can combine the "hear" and "see" steps. This happens when you are explaining and watching how to do a certain skill.

Do: The next step is doing. Once you've heard how to do it and seen it done firsthand, then you're ready to try it yourself. This is the real test of whether or not you actually learned what you heard. Sometimes you might have to try something several times before you get it. That's normal.

Teach: When you've learned a new skill, the best way to make sure you know it is to teach it to others. Try to teach someone what you have learned, soon after you learn it. That helps others grow and learn, and it helps you remember what you have been taught.

A commonly held idea claims that a person who only hears how to do a skill has a low retention of the skill. If he also sees the skill being demonstrated, his retention increases. If he then actually does the skill after receiving verbal and visual instructions, his retention increases again. But if he teaches the skill he has been working on, his retention reaches a high level. Clearly, your knowledge of a subject will be much greater if you are involved in teaching the material to others.

In Rangers, you will get the chance to teach skills to new members and other Rangers. Use the "hear, see, do, teach" method. You'll learn more and help others learn more too.

Uniforms

Guys want to belong to a community of great men. They want to be friends, have fun together, and encourage each other. Part of that involves what what we wear. In Rangers, we have the gear you need. And it has a look and feel your group will be comfortable with.

Sports teams and other groups use uniforms. Uniforms can help you pick out players, coaches, and fans. Uniforms also promote the group to your community. In Rangers, uniforms can help you feel like you're part of the group. And they can help your group present its own image.

Uniform Options

Every leader, boy, and young man in Royal Rangers is encouraged to wear a uniform. Your local outpost can pick the uniform options that work best for your group. The option your outpost picks will be welcomed at all events. Talk to your leader about your outpost's choices. You can find uniform guidelines at Royal-Rangers.com. (Ask your parents before going online.)

Your outpost may pick from the options that follow.

Utility Uniform

The utility uniform is a balance between a dress uniform and more activewear. The utility uniform has these parts:

Shirt: official utility shirt, worn in either patch or pin format. The pin format allows you to wear patches and pins. It is for more formal events. You may not wear pins with the patch format. See RoyalRangers.com for details.

Pants: official Rangers tactical pants and web belt, jeans, or knee-length shorts

You may wear an undershirt. It may be of any color and sleeve length. Many Rangers wear their awards vest over their utility shirt. You must wear a bolo tie when the utility shirt is tucked in. The bolo tie is optional when the utility shirt is not tucked in. There are several hats you can pick from. Wear proper shoes for the activity.

> **Full uniform information and guidelines**
> **are available at RoyalRangers.com.**
> **See also Appendix B, page 187.**

Special Uniform

Your group may pick the special uniform. Special uniforms can take lots of forms. They may include special clothing items that display the Royal Rangers logo, your outpost number, and district name. Examples of special uniforms include casual pants (such as blue jeans or shorts), and a polo shirt, T-shirt, sports jersey, or hoodie. Hats and shoes for special uniforms are whatever your outpost picks.

Awards Vest

You can wear your awards vest as a special uniform or as a supplement to another uniform option. The awards vest gives you an ideal way to display awards, training patches, and event patches you've earned in your current age group.

Uniform Rules

Royal Rangers has many attractive and comfortable clothing options. This makes it easy to pick a uniform that matches the style your outpost has selected.

To maintain consistency and to protect the image of Royal Rangers, please observe the following rules when wearing uniforms.

- Wear patches, pins, and other insignia only on utility uniforms and the awards vest. Do not wear patches and insignia on a special uniform.

- Comply with official national uniform standards and insignia placement rules. Wear only approved insignia. Check the national Royal Rangers Web site or books to see what has been approved.

- Special guidelines are available at RoyalRangers.com for official color/honor guard uniform items. Only the accessory items in these guidelines may be worn on the Royal Rangers uniform. They are used only during special color guard ceremonies.

Some restrictions apply to the use of the Royal Rangers name and emblems. Visit RoyalRangers.com for details concerning our trademarks use policy.

VISIT THE RANGERS ONLINE SUPERSTORE

www.RoyalRangers.com

Rangers uniform apparel and accessories
can be purchased from the Rangers Online
Superstore at www.RoyalRangers.com
or by calling 1-800-641-4310.

The Patrol System

The patrol system is a method of outpost leadership where you participate in leading the experiences of your group in Royal Rangers. Patrols usually have three to eight Rangers. Being part of a patrol helps you develop as a leader. There are at least five good reasons to be part of a patrol.

You Will Do Fun Things with Friends

One of the biggest reasons is friendship. The guys in a patrol usually are already friends or know each other. You may attend the same school. Or, you may live in the same neighborhood. Being in Royal Ranges is more fun when your friends are there. You can invite your friends to be in Royal Rangers. And the patrol system is a great way to make new friends!

You Are Important

You are part of a small group—three to eight Discovery Rangers—and everyone counts. You have a chance to get involved. You need everyone in the patrol to do something. That way everyone has a chance to be important. If your outpost has patrols, you will always be with a group who knows what you can do. They will need you. So, you won't get lost in the crowd, no matter how big the outpost is.

You Have a Job to Do

Maybe you've never thought of yourself as a leader. The patrol system gives a chance to be one. Every patrol needs a patrol leader. The patrol also needs an assistant patrol leader, a communications specialist, and a gear manager. There are also other positions of responsibility. All these jobs give you a chance to lead in some way. Whether you are a natural leader or not, you deserve a chance to show what you can do. You also deserve a chance to improve.

You Get to Be a Participant

Did you know that when you and the other Rangers step up and lead, your adult leaders can spend time doing other things? It's true. The more your patrol can do for itself, the more your adult leaders can mentor, counsel, coach, and troubleshoot problems too big for you to handle. Don't let or expect your adult leaders to do everything for you. The only way to grow as a leader is to do as much as you can.

You Develop Leadership Skills

A patrol is run as a democracy. You get to elect your patrol leader. The patrol leader represents your patrol on the Group Leadership Team (GLT). The GLT plans and runs the group program. The senior patrol leader is the chairman of the GLT. Adult leaders provide oversight and direction to the GLT.

The GLT is made up of all the adult and boy leaders from your age group. These leaders plan the weekly meetings and group outings. You should elect a new patrol leader at least twice a year so more guys can serve as a patrol leader.

One More Time

Let's look at these reasons again.

- **Friends.** Patrols allow a Ranger to be in the same group as his friends and make new friends.

- **Small size.** Using patrols means all guys get involved because all are really needed.

- **Responsibility.** Patrol jobs for everyone means all get a chance to learn and practice responsibility.

- **Adult leaders are helped.** The more you can do yourself, the less your adult leaders must do.

- **Leadership.** Patrols provide experience in being a servant leader.

What a Dynamic Patrol Looks Like

One great thing about Royal Rangers is that great patrols do not all look alike. Your patrol will have its own unique identity. You, as a patrol member, have a say in that identity. But there are some common traits found in great patrols. Let's look at some of these.

Patrol Identity

Every patrol needs a name. Pick a special name. Make sure the name describes a quality or characteristic you want. The name may have a long tradition. Or, it may be new and never before used. Whatever it is, it gives each member a special way to identify themselves.

Make sure your patrol name is exciting. Don't just call yourselves the Eagle or Steel Patrol but the "Screaming Eagles" or "Forged Steel." Make it something everyone will be proud of.

Now that you have a patrol name, use it! There are many ways to use the patrol name to build patrol spirit. Put the name on a patrol flag or banner. Use it in a song or yell. You can even make a special patrol emblem or logo that you can put on your patrol gear. The important thing is to use your patrol name.

Activity

All patrols need to be active. Outdoor activities, field trips, and contests are great ways for your patrol to be active. Leadership training and service projects work too. Most activities will be with your group or outpost. So, other patrols will be there as well.

You may plan some activities just for your patrol. There are a few rules. You need your group leader's consent. Next, a patrol activity can't get in the way of a group or outpost activity. Also, every activity requires adult control. Safety guidelines must be followed.

Purpose

One of the reasons to use patrols is to share leadership. Everyone gets a chance to lead. That means listening to ideas from other guys. If one person gets his way all the time, it probably isn't fun for others. The more you allow other guys to take the lead in something, the more fun it will be for everyone especially if they can do things they are good at. It is important to find out what the others do well and how they can make the patrol better.

The patrol system allows you do fun things with friends and sometimes even make mistakes. Some mistakes are okay. Some aren't. Having a safe place to make mistakes is important. Some mistakes are lessons you will never forget. These can make you develop into a better leader. Always try to learn from your mistakes.

Goals

Successful patrols learn how to set and reach goals. Use the SMART goals outline from the Junior Leadership Foundations material. Here's a brief description. SMART goals are:

- **S**pecific: Goals need to be clear. Everyone needs to be able to understand and support them.

- **M**easurable: Measurements show you have achieved the goal.

- **A**chievable: Goals need to be reasonable.

- **R**esults-focused: Goals must result in change or improvement, not just keeping people busy. What specific activities will we do to get results?

- **T**ime-sensitive: Goals need to have a time limit.

Here is an example of a SMART goal: We will grow our patrol from four to eight members. Each of us will recruit one new member to join in the next three months.

- We will grow our patrol. That is specific.

- We will measure our success when we have grown from four to eight members.

- We can achieve this. It is not wishful thinking.

- We define our activities that will get results. Each person is to recruit one new member.

- We define our time frame by saying it will be done within three months.

Always write your SMART goals. That way they will serve as your leadership road map. Follow them, and you'll get places. As the saying goes, "Plan your work, and work your plan!"

What are some goals your patrol might pursue? Your group might want to raise a certain amount of money or grow by a certain number of members. Or, maybe you want to work on a service project that will help your church. Whatever the goal, make it a SMART goal. Nothing makes Rangers more fun than making things happen! (A great goal to achieve is to earn the Patrol of Excellence Medallion. See chapter 19 for details.)

Belonging

It's great to know you have a place where you are valued and accepted. It's great to have a place where you can get help even when you mess up. In a patrol, everyone has value and can add something to the group. You can share your ideas and take on new challenges knowing you are not doing it alone. You can make new friends and do fun things.

Growth

The more you grow as a junior leader and Christlike young man, the stronger your group and outpost becomes. It's true. As you become more skilled and confident, you can assume more responsibility in the patrol and group. You will be able to lead and influence others. You will also become an example to younger Rangers.

You may also take a greater and greater role in planning and conducting outpost meetings, activities, and projects. The more experienced junior leaders a group has, the stronger it becomes. The stronger the group is, the more boys and young men it can influence for Christ.

So to put it all together, a great patrol has an identity to be proud of. It's very active, but it does things with a purpose. It knows how to set and accomplish goals. A great patrol is a group where members feel accepted and add value to the team. A great patrol is one in which everyone is growing as a leader and as a godly young man.

> *"Leadership is the art of getting someone else to do something you want done because he wants to do it."*
>
> *Dwight D. Eisenhower*

Leadership Positions and Responsibilities

Royal Rangers allows you to lead. This helps you learn to impact others in a helpful way. To develop as a leader, fill a variety of roles in your group. This chapter will let you know about lots of leadership jobs you can fill.

All leadership positions in the group have some common traits no matter what your title may be. Here are some important ones to work on.

Setting a Christlike example in thought, word, and deed at all times is a responsibility of every junior leader. This could be tough, but it is a goal you can achieve with God's help. Examples of the kinds of behaviors junior leaders need to show might include:

- Living by the Royal Rangers Motto, Pledge, and Code and being ready to recite them.

- Being able to explain the meaning of the Royal Rangers Emblem whenever asked.

- Working with other outpost leaders to ensure the outpost functions well.

- Setting the standard by aggressively continuing to earn merits and advancements, and encouraging others to do the same.

- Completing and assisting in junior leadership training.

- Encouraging all outpost members to participate in district and national events.

- Encouraging Rangers to actively participate in service projects.

- Actively participating in and attending outpost, group, and patrol activities and events.

- Wearing the outpost's prescribed Royal Rangers uniform proudly and correctly.

- Enthusiastically showing Royal Rangers spirit.

Each position has someone you report to. This is the person who helps you learn how to do your job. He will help and coach you when you need it. Every good leader values this kind of assistance.

Each leadership job has a time limit. Often you will serve for six months in a job. This allows you time to learn how to lead in that area and gain vital knowledge and practice before taking a new job. However, your group leaders may make job terms longer or shorter.

All jobs have conditions you must meet before you can serve. These let you know what you must to do to qualify for a certain job. Set your goals based on what you must do to qualify for jobs you want in the future. Some jobs may require you to be a certain age or grade. You may also be required to have a certain advancement level and length of service in the outpost. In a new outpost, leaders can be picked for a short time and new leaders chosen at the end of a given period.

Patrol Leadership
Let's take a look at the patrol leadership roles in most outposts.

Patrol Leader

Patrol members usually pick their leaders. If you earn their vote, it means the rest of the patrol believes you will be a good leader.

PATROL LEADER

"How do I do my job?" This question is often asked by new patrol leaders. First of all, congratulations! What a great chance to lead! Being a patrol leader can be exciting. It can also be challenging and very rewarding. You will be the one to lead the other Rangers in the patrol. They will be looking to you for guidance and direction. Other adult and junior leaders will be expecting you to do your best. They want you to succeed, so you can count on their help. So here is your chance to make a difference and help your patrol and outpost grow, have fun, and make its mark on your church and community. And don't forget, you can count on God to help you!

Specific patrol leader duties are:

- Plan and lead your group's meetings and activities.
- Keep patrol members informed about group news and events.
- Appoint members to patrol jobs and help them learn to do their jobs right.
- Represent your patrol at all Group Leadership Team meetings and at the annual planning conference.
- Help your patrol get ready to take part in all outpost/group activities.
- Promote patrol spirit.
- Gently push others to earn their merits.
- Do the Junior Leadership Foundations interview for your assistant patrol leader.
- Report to the senior patrol leader.

It is suggested that patrol leaders have a Gold Falcon award, a year of service in the outpost, and be least nine years old.

Assistant Patrol Leader

The patrol leader (PL) picks the assistant patrol leader (APL). If you are the assistant patrol leader, you lead the patrol if the patrol leader is absent. You and the patrol leader should talk about the rest of the patrol jobs before they are assigned. Once those are assigned, you get to conduct the Junior Leadership Foundation interviews. The patrol leader may assist you if needed. You also train each of those Rangers and supervise them in their jobs.

Specific duties of the assistant patrol leader are:

- Assume the duties of the patrol leader in his absence.
- Help the patrol leader with his duties.
- Represent the patrol at Group Leadership Team meetings if the patrol leader can't be there.
- Work with the other leaders to make the group run well.
- Earn merits and advancements so others will.
- Talk with the patrol leader about whom to assign patrol jobs to.
- Conduct Junior Leadership Foundations interviews for the other leaders in your patrol.
- Other duties as needed.
- Report to the patrol leader.

It is suggested that assistant patrol leaders have at least a year of service in the outpost.

Patrol Communications Specialist

If the patrol leader picks you for communications specialist, you are responsible for communications within the patrol.

Specific patrol communications specialist duties are:

- Keep notes of patrol meetings and report on those notes as needed.
- Keep a record of who attends the meetings and collect dues.
- Keep a record of how to contact each patrol member.
- Provide news about your patrol for group leaders to share.
- Promote events.
- Keep records of points for the Patrol of Excellence awards.
- Other duties as needed.
- Report to the assistant patrol leader.

It is suggested that candidates for this job have at least a year of service in the outpost.

Patrol Gear Manager

If the patrol leader picks you for gear manager, you will keep a list about the patrol's gear. You should keep a list of the gear the group has. Your record should show the condition of the gear. You get and return outpost gear needed by the patrol. The outpost gear manager oversees gear owned by the entire outpost. You also make sure everyone in the patrol has what he needs for each event.

Specific gear manager duties are:

- Help maintain all the patrol gear.
- Make sure that outpost gear is in good condition when it's returned.
- Work with the outpost gear manager and the outpost committee member who oversees the group's gear.
- Other duties as needed.
- Report to the assistant patrol leader.

It is suggested that the gear manager have been part of the outpost for at least a year.

Event Planner

The patrol leader picks the event planner. If you are chosen for this job, you will plan patrol events and activities. You will make a schedule, a menu, and lists of supplies and gear needed for events and activities. This is a vital job! It's all about the details.

Specific event planner job duties are:

- Help plan activities and events.
- Keep files of what is needed for planning and conducting activities. Things to put in the files are schedules, maps, brochures, and menus.

- Other duties as needed.

- Report to the assistant patrol leader.

It is suggested that guys who fill this job have at least a year of service to the outpost.

Spirit Leader

The patrol leader picks the spirit leader. If you are the spirit leader, you are in charge of promoting patrol spirit and keeping up morale.

Specific spirit leader duties are:

- In charge of the overall spirit of the patrol. The patrol and group will set guidelines for how you manage the group's morale.

- Learn and teach the patrol songs. You may also be required to teach yells, stunts, and event programs.

- Develop and improve patrol symbols. Patrol symbols are the patrol name, nickname, standard or banner, logo, T-shirt, bolo, etc.

- Other duties as needed.

- Report to the assistant patrol leader.

It is suggested that the spirit leader have a year of service in the outpost.

Other Positions

The patrol jobs listed here are suggestions. Other jobs can be assigned if they are needed.

Group Leadership

Now let's talk about how you can lead at the group level. The following junior leader jobs may be available to you: senior patrol leader, assistant senior patrol leader, communications specialist, gear manager, historian, and chaplain aide. Each group can have its own leadership team. But sometimes that does not work. A small outpost may have a leadership team for all three groups. Or, it may have something in between. The main thing is to make the system work for your outpost. Guys who are already known to be developing good leadership skills often fill these jobs. If you're not quite there yet, set goals for yourself and start working to reach them. These guys help train the patrol leaders. They help the outpost run smoothly.

Senior Patrol Leader

Senior patrol leaders have the top job in the group. They also have the toughest job. If you have that job, your adult group leader picked you for it. That means your peers respect you and the adult leaders feel you can run the group.

SENIOR PATROL LEADER

As you lead and gain more skill and confidence, you grow as a leader. What's more, as you earn the respect of others, your role in the outpost will increase as well. Your primary job is to grow as a leader yourself and help other boys to become leaders too. You must learn to delegate tasks. Don't try to do it all yourself.

As senior patrol leader you are not a member of a patrol. Your duties include these:

- With the help of your group leader, preside over group meetings, Group Leadership Team meetings, events, activities, and the annual planning retreat.

- Appoint the assistant senior patrol leader. The group leader will help.

- Appoint the following positions with input from the assistant senior patrol leader: group communications specialist, outpost gear manager, and historian. (The chaplain approves the selection of the chaplain aide.)

- Assign duties to the assistant senior patrol leader. Ensure he attends meetings/functions you cannot attend.

- Assist the assistant senior patrol leader in training other leaders.

- Oversee group planning activities and events even if you cannot attend.

- Conduct Junior Leadership Foundations interviews for assistant senior patrol leader and for patrol leaders.

- Promote the Patrol of Excellence awards.

- Report to the group leader.

It is suggested that those who fill this job have earned a Gold Hawk award. It is also suggested that they have a year of service in the outpost, display solid Christian character, be faithful in church attendance, correctly wear the preferred uniform of your group, and be at least ten years of age.

Newer outposts may need to ease these standards until they can be met. Established outposts may make them tougher. After all, the senior patrol leader plays an important role. A top junior leader should fill this role. A smart and healthy outpost will develop several junior leaders who can be senior patrol leader.

Assistant Senior Patrol Leader

If you are the assistant senior patrol leader (ASPL), welcome to

leadership. You are the second-highest ranking junior leader in the group. The senior patrol leader picked you. But the group leader had to approve the choice. You do the senior patrol leader's job when he is absent, or if you are asked. You also guide other junior leaders

ASST. SENIOR PATROL LEADER

in the outpost. An assistant senior patrol leader is not a member of a patrol.

Specific assistant senior patrol leader duties include these:

- Assume the job duties of the senior patrol leader if he is absent.
- Help lead meetings and activities.
- Help the senior patrol leader appoint, train, and supervise the following junior leaders: group communications specialist, gear manager, and historian.
- Conduct Junior Leadership Foundations interviews of the group communications specialist, gear manager, and historian.
- Do what the senior patrol leader asks.
- Serve on the Group Leadership Team.
- Other duties as needed.
- Report to the senior patrol leader.

It is suggested that those who fill this job have earned a Gold Hawk award, one year of service in the outpost, display solid Christian character, be faithful in church attendance, correctly wear the preferred uniform of your group, and be at least ten years of age.

Group Communications Specialist

If the senior patrol leader picks you for communications specialist, you will keep outpost records. And you will give news to the other group members. You will work with a member of the Outpost Committee. You are a member of a patrol.

COMMUNICATIONS SPECIALIST

Specific group communications specialist duties include these:

- Serve on the Group Leadership Team. Keep notes about its meetings.

- Keep attendance records and collect dues.

- Keep a record that shows how to contact group members.

- Help with the outpost Web site, social network utility, and outpost newsletter.

- Promote events.

- Report to the assistant senior patrol leader.

It is suggested that guys who fill this job have a year of service in the outpost.

Group Gear Manager

If the senior patrol leader picks you for gear manager, you will help manage the supplies and gear, along with the patrol gear managers and the adult leaders. You will work with a member of the Outpost Committee. You are a member of a patrol.

Specific gear manager duties include these:

- Keep an inventory of group gear.

- Assist in making sure the gear is in proper shape when it's checked in after use.

- Work with the patrol gear managers.

- Tell the Group Leadership Team about gear needing major repair or replacement.

- Work with an Outpost Committee member to repair gear and purchase new gear as needed.

- Report to the assistant senior patrol leader.

It is suggested that guys who fill this job have a year of service in the outpost.

Group Historian

If the senior patrol leader picks you for historian, you will care for group memorabilia and keep a historical record of group activities. Be part of keeping the legacy of your outpost alive. You are a member of a patrol. Specific duties of the historian include these:

- Gather pictures and facts about past outpost activities.
- Develop a memory book, wall displays, online or informational (historical) files etc.
- Take care of group trophies, ribbons, and souvenirs of activities.
- Keep information about former members of the group.
- Other duties as assigned by the outpost leadership.
- Report to the assistant senior patrol leader.

It is suggested that guys who fill this job have a year of service in the outpost.

Chaplain Aide

If the chaplain picks you to be the chaplain aide, you will work with the chaplain to meet the spiritual needs of the group. This is a great job if you feel a call to ministry. You are a member of a patrol.

Specific duties of the chaplain aide include these:

- Assist the chaplain.

- Display a growing spiritual walk with God.

- Under the chaplain's supervision, prepare and present devotions and Bible studies.

- Be ready to present the salvation message as opportunities present themselves and prompted by the Holy Spirit.

- Report to the chaplain.

It is suggested that guys who fill this job have a year of service in the outpost and feel a call from God to ministry.

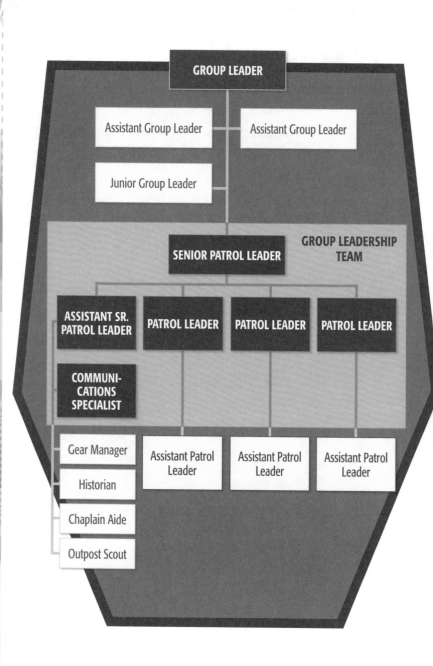

*"You are
the body of Christ,
and each one of you
is a part of it."*

1 Corinthians 12:27

The Group Leadership Team

The Group Leadership Team (GLT) is probably Royal Rangers' best example of junior leaders in action. This is where Discovery Rangers get to help lead their group. They have help and coaching from adult leaders. Let's see how it works.

Who Makes Up the GLT?

The senior patrol leader and assistant senior patrol leader are on the Group Leadership Team. The patrol leaders from each patrol and the group communications specialist are part of the GLT, too. The group leader, assistant group leaders, and the junior group leaders serve as advisors. This team works together to plan and run the program. Each patrol leader is to present the view of his patrol to the GLT. Also he must tell his patrol about the plans and choices the team makes.

In this way, every Ranger has a voice in running the outpost. The Group Leadership Team is a great place for patrol leaders to get on-the-job training.

The Group Leadership Team should meet regularly. Most teams meet once every two or three months. Your team should pick the option that works best for it. GLT meetings help groups stay focused on the interests of the guys in the group. Keep it fun! The Group Leadership Team helps prepare for activities and meetings. Good planning makes good events!

What Do GLT Meetings Look Like?

The senior patrol leader and his group leader plan the agenda. To plan the agenda, review the agenda from the last meeting. You'll find it in the records kept by the communications specialist. Think about what was discussed, what was settled, and what wasn't settled. Then determine what new items should be discussed.

The senior patrol leader runs the Group Leadership Team meeting with the help of the group leader. If the senior patrol leader cannot attend, the assistant senior patrol leader takes charge. Schedule meetings so that most members of the GLT can attend. Be aware of possible problems. Avoid holidays, major church events, and other conflicts.

Relaxed, unplanned meetings can happen anytime GLT members are in the same place. A five-minute chat after a weekly meeting can be useful. It's a great way to make sure all leaders will be ready for the next meeting. Keep these meetings short.

Sometimes other junior leaders are asked to sit in a GLT meeting. Often this is when their areas of knowledge are likely to be discussed. Here's how it all fits together.

1. Opening: The senior patrol leader calls the meeting to order. He greets everyone. He invites a member of the team to pray for the meeting. Review notes from other meetings if needed.

2. Patrol reports: Patrol leaders tell what their patrols have done since the last meeting.

3. Old business: Discuss matters not finished at the last meeting. This is also the time for members to report on things they were asked to do.

4. New business: The group talks about new items.

5. Advancement: Study advancement reports. Look at your goals for progress on merits for the quarter and the year. Plan advancement opportunities.

6. Program planning: The GLT reviews weekly meeting plans. It also looks at assigned duties. You should also talk about activities and projects that are related to the quarterly program.

7. Group leader's time: This takes place after the business is done. The group leader will have a brief time to make comments. He will end with an uplifting and challenging thought from the Bible. The meeting ends in prayer.

8. Meeting review: The senior patrol leader and group leader should talk briefly. This is to tie up loose ends. You also want to make sure nothing on the agenda was missed. This is a good time for the senior patrol leader to get some coaching. You all win when everyone has a part in running the outpost! And, it won't take you long to realize this.

Annual Planning Retreat

Each year, your group leader and senior patrol leader help the Group Leadership Team set goals for the next year. The goals may be events, service projects, and merits that guys want to earn. The GLT will make and present a plan to the outpost and church leaders for approval. Before the retreat, GLT members should talk to their patrols. That way, they know what their patrols want to do. The work of the GLT at the retreat puts the fun into Royal Rangers!

Being a member of the GLT is a big honor and duty. You get to serve your fellow Rangers and help make their experience the best it can be. So with God's help, do your best to serve your group and your outpost well.

Ask your group leader
if he has access to the most
recent Royal Rangers'
online resources.

Available anywhere,
anytime on the Internet.

TRaCclub.org offers great
weekly meeting plans,
merits, and more.

Leading Group Meetings

The senior patrol leader leads the weekly meetings and activities with the help of the group leader. He counts on the patrol leaders and members to help. This isn't a one-man show. The other junior leaders should run meetings and activities as much as possible. Don't expect adults to do what junior leaders can do themselves. Let's walk through a meeting. That way you can see how to be involved. A well-rounded meeting will be fun. It will give you and everyone else a real sense of success.

1. **While the Boys Arrive:** This is the time just before the meeting starts. It can be from ten minutes to thirty minutes. This is when the junior leaders and the group leader review the meeting plan. Other junior leaders should be setting up for the meeting. It is also a good time to greet everyone. Be sure to greet anyone new to the group. You may also use an activity to keep others busy until it's time to start.

2. **Opening Ceremony:** Junior leaders open the meeting. The Opening Ceremony can include pledges, the Code, worship, a video, quick demonstrations, etc. Make a good first impression. Be creative. Use lots of openings. A good opening starts on time and includes prayer. It is also brief.

3. **Business/Patrol Corners:** This is when your patrol gets to work together. The patrol leader runs this part of the meeting. You can plan projects and events during this time. You should also welcome visitors. This is the right time to take attendance, collect dues, and make announcements.

4. **Bible Study:** This is a key part of every meeting. Each Bible merit is designed to help you reach mature, godly manhood. Lessons should be lead by a pastor, the chaplain aide, chaplain, a group leader, or a confident junior leader.

5. **Program Feature:** This is when you do skill merits. They may be taught by junior or adult leaders. Sometimes skill merits prepare you for a group or outpost activity.

6. **Advancement:** Your group leaders or someone they trust will sign off on advancement requirements you have finished.

7. **Recreation:** Each meeting has recreation time. This is scheduled fun. Junior leaders should run this part of the meeting. Don't wear out a favorite game by playing it too often. Try new games. You may find a new favorite!

8. **Devotion:** This is a great time to connect with God and let Him speak to you. These are often lead by a pastor, the chaplain aide, chaplain, a group leader, or a confident junior leader.

9. **Closing Ceremony:** This is when you wrap up. As much as possible, match your theme. Keep it brief. End the meeting in prayer.

10. **After the Meeting:** Make sure the room is clean and orderly. It's also a good time to talk with members of the Group Leadership Team. You can get feedback on the meeting. You can also review plans and duties for future meetings and events. This should only take about five minutes.

So, there you have it. A good meeting keeps things moving and uses a lot of junior leaders. You can get a lot done and have fun too. The same principles apply to patrol and group activities. The key is that you and the other junior leaders should lead as much as you can. After all, Royal Rangers is all about finding ways to let you lead yourself and others!

Trip Planning

In Royal Rangers, you will have fun, active meetings. You will get out and do things! Plan events and activities that involve outdoor skills, sports, technology, trades, arts and ministry. Great outposts plan a wide variety of activities. The key word is *planning*. Just like you need to plan for great meetings, you need to plan your events.

Do you have some great ideas for activities? Share your ideas and help plan the events. The Group Leadership Team needs your input. After all, these activities are for you.

Key Questions

Good planning will require answering key questions like these:

What is it, and where can you do it?

This is an easy one. Decide what your activity is and where you want to do it.

When are you leaving and returning?

Date and time to leave and return is needed so you all get there and back on time. This is vital information everyone needs to know. This also means you will need to know how long it takes to get there. Is there an opening and closing time? How long will you be there?

Who is going?

Make a list of Rangers and adults going. You need to know how many in order to plan transportation, food, equipment, etc. Do you need people with special certifications or skills? Also, it is important to leave a list of who is going with an adult not attending the event in case there is a delay or an emergency. One call to that person, and he can contact all the right people.

Why are you going?

Every activity and trip should have a purpose. Is it for learning new skills, outreach, advancements, or preparing for another event? Make sure you plan for fun, but put God first. Make time for devotions, Scripture reading, worship, prayer, and inviting God to be an important part of every Rangers event.

What do you need?

You don't want to go somewhere and realize you needed something you didn't bring. Plan ahead and think things through carefully. Will you need special equipment, clothing, permits, maps, permission forms, training, bad weather gear, money for fees, food, etc. Prepare for the obvious and plan for the unexpected. A Ranger is "ready for anything," right?

How to . . . ?

This last question is open-ended but very important. "How to" will help you figure out how you will get there and back; how to do something safely; how much it will cost and how to pay for it; how to get it on the church calendar and promote it; how to reserve a church van, etc. Don't ignore these questions! The small things can make a big difference.

As you can see, asking and answering the right questions is the key to having great events and activities. Don't wait until the last minute to ask these questions. Make good plans! Do it early; don't put it off. Plan with others; don't do it alone. Share responsibilities; don't make the event a one-man show. And like most other skills, the more you plan the easier it gets and the more you will grow as a leader. You'll enjoy being a team member who makes things happen!

Patrol of Excellence

How do you know if you are part of a great patrol? One way is to see how you match up to the Patrol of Excellence guidelines. The Patrol of Excellence award is for active patrols. To earn this honor, patrols must make good use of the patrol system. Patrols earn points based on the guidelines. The patrols are presented the proper medallions each quarter. You can display the medallions in your group's meeting room. This lets everyone know that each guy gives his best effort.

Each patrol that earns more than 1,000 points in the quarter is a gold level patrol. Groups that earn between 900 and 999 points get silver recognition. Groups between 800 and 899 points get bronze. Your patrol starts with no points. You want to reach gold each quarter. Here are the suggested guidelines:

1. Patrol Spirit

- Use an attractive patrol logo. The logo may be used on shirts, flags, banners, or gear, etc. at patrol and group activities. This is worth one hundred points.

- Maintain patrol records during the quarter. Records should include attendance, merits finished, and patrol meeting notes. This is worth one hundred points.

- Maintain a memory book, scrapbook, or photo album. This is worth one hundred points.

- Design or give content to and use a patrol, group, or outpost Web page. This is worth fifty points.

- Set up, give content to, or help maintain an outpost Internet newsgroup or social utility. This should help keep guys in the patrol informed. This is worth fifty points.

2. Patrol Meetings

- Plan and hold patrol meetings. Your group gets twenty-five points for each meeting held during the quarter.

- If the patrol leader or assistant patrol leader is at all Group Leadership Team meetings in the quarter, the group gets one hundred points.

3. Activities

- Participate in activities. This includes national, district, or sectional events. Outpost activities count, too. Outpost activities are things like hikes, camps, and sporting events.

Patrol activities approved by the senior patrol leader and the group leader also count. Your group gets 150 points for each event.

4. Service Projects

• Participate as a patrol in a church-approved service project. Your group gets 150 points for each project.

5. Advancement

• Your patrol gets fifty points if at least half the guys earn the quarterly advancement step.

• Your patrol gets one hundred points if at least two-thirds of the guys earn the quarterly advancement step.

• Your patrol gets two hundred points if all the members complete the quarterly advancement step.

NOTE: A patrol can only earn points at only one level. A patrol cannot earn points at two or more levels.

6. Uniform

• Your group gets one hundred points if at least two-thirds of the guys wear the group's preferred uniform to all events.

• Your group gets two hundred points if all guys wear the group's preferred uniform to all outpost events.

NOTE: A patrol can only earn points at only one level. A patrol cannot earn points at two or more levels.

7. Annual Group Planning Retreat

• Your group gets two hundred points if the patrol leader or the assistant patrol leader is at the yearly group planning retreat.

Okay, so here is the challenge. Use the Patrol of Excellence for all your patrols, if you are not already doing so. See if you have what it takes to be a gold level patrol!

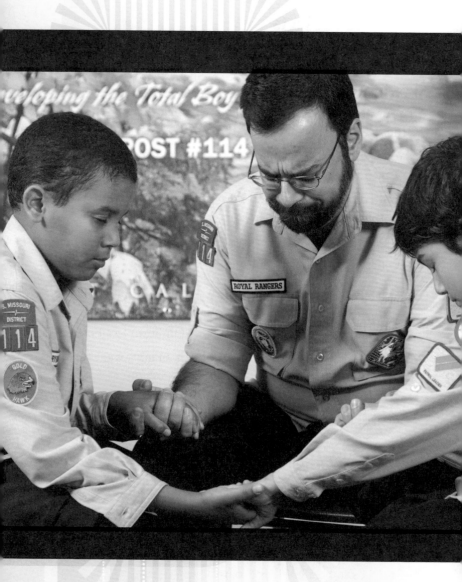

Junior Leadership Development

You have lots of opportunities to learn and develop as a leader. In Royal Rangers, the process involves experiencing leadership in your own outpost and at special functions offered in your own district. You will love the challenge! Here's how it works.

Local Leadership Training

The local leadership training cycle is a two-step process.

Junior Leadership Foundations

When you are elected or appointed to a leadership position in your patrol, your group leader or another member of your group will get you started by meeting with you and walking you through the Junior Leadership Foundations (JLF) materials. This is what it involves.

First, you will participate in an introduction to leadership interview for about ten to fifteen minutes. You will be assigned an achievable goal that you can complete within one week.

Second, you will be asked to read some information from this handbook so you are ready to succeed at your new job.

Lastly, you will be asked to show your interviewer your group's uniform. As a junior leader, it is important you wear your uniform consistently and correctly according to national guidelines. By wearing your uniform correctly, you inspire a sense of belonging and pride in the group, in your district, and across the nation.

Once you have knocked out these three requirements, you will receive the Junior Leadership Foundations patch and certificate as recognition for your accomplishment.

Leadership Merits

About every six months, your group leader will teach a new leadership merit. At times he may do this during the regular weekly meetings. At other times, he may take the group out for a weekend learning about leadership.

Each merit lesson will give you really good leadership information. The lessons will include fun and interactive games and activities to reinforce what you have learned. It will be fun! Finally, you will gain a sense of accomplishment by practicing servant leadership as you complete a service project with your group.

Your main handbook for earning leadership merits is the book *A Guy's Journey to Servant Leadership*. This book includes all the leadership distinctives used in earning leadership merits.

Copies of this book can be purchased at RoyalRangers.com (item 02-0619).

District Leadership Training

While the local outpost is the primary place and means of developing junior leaders, you can also rely on help from your district. The training events offered by the district will complement your local training. The big benefit is you will be interacting with junior leaders from others outposts. Here is what is offered in a typical district.

Merit Camps

Merit camps are special events usually conducted by your district once each year. These camps typically allow you to earn merits your local outpost may not be able to offer.

Junior Leadership Training Camps

These camps reinforce and expand on the training you receive in your outpost. There is time to learn and lots of time to have fun with your friends from around the district. Most important, you will be inspired in your relationship with God. Discovery Rangers may attend Ranger Training Camp (RTC). This camp provides in-depth training on how to use the patrol system in the outpost.

Action Camps

Action Camps are for the adult leaders and Expedition Rangers from your outpost. They learn to lead new and different Ranger activities and return to the outpost ready to share what they have learned with the rest of the guys. These camps are something to look forward to when you reach Expedition Rangers.

Trail of the Saber

The Trail of the Saber award is designed for those who take full advantage of the junior leadership development opportunities available in their outpost and district. Upon completion of the requirements, Expedition Rangers are eligible for a special nationally restricted medal. The award acknowledges your servant leadership development that starts in Discovery or Adventure Rangers and culminates while you are an Expedition Ranger.

"Don't let anyone look down on you because you are young, but set an example for the believers in speech, in conduct, in love, in faith and in purity."

1 Timothy 4:12

Service: It's What Rangers Do!

In Royal Rangers, you will do things that help you learn to act like Jesus. The life of Christ is the model for moving from boyhood to godly manhood. Nothing illustrates the life of Jesus more than His desire to serve.

Chapter 21

Serving others and living with a servant's heart isn't something you do just once. It isn't something you do just when it's easy. It's something that should be normal for a follower of Jesus. To develop the heart of a servant you will have to rethink many things. Servants put others first.

There are many ways to serve others. Be on the lookout to help people. When you serve others you are serving Jesus. Be spontaneous and help when you see a need. You should also plan ahead and be intentional in your service to others.

> **"Serve wholeheartedly, as if you were serving the Lord, not people"**
> **(Ephesians 6:7).**

Take a look at the following chart.

WAYS TO SERVE	PERSONAL	GROUP
Spontaneous	Personally serving others at the moment of learning of a need. • Mowing the lawn of a sick neighbor • Helping an elderly person across the street	Doing service for someone as a group at the moment of learning the need. • Helping someone move after church • Moving someone's vehicle that has broken down
Planned	Planning to serve others after discovering a need. • Visiting the sick in the hospital • Serving at a soup kitchen	Planning a group event to serve others after learning of a need. • Outreach to the community, a school, or a missions trip • Making repairs on an elderly person's home

Here are some intentional and meaningful ways you can get involved in serving others.

Missions Support

A great way for Ranger Kids and Discovery Rangers to serve is by giving money to Boys and Girls Missionary Challenge (BGMC). Older Rangers can give money to Speed the Light (STL). These ministries help missionaries around the world.

Visit RoyalRangers.com for more information on BGMC and Speed the Light.

Outreach

You may also help with missions trips or local outreach activities. Ministries such as PathFinder Missions, Ambassadors in Mission (AIM), and Convoy of Hope let Rangers help. The Missions Project Award is for boys, young men, or leaders involved in missions trips. Details for the Missions Project Award are online at RoyalRangers.com.

More information on ministries can be found at their Web site:

pathfindermissions.com

aim.ag.org

convoyofhope.org

MEGASportscamp.com

MEGA Sports Camp events can be a great way to share the gospel with your area. Ranger Derby rallies can draw people from the community to your church.

Service is a basic element of the Christlike life. It is a lifestyle, not just an event. The service you render to others will benefit them. But it will help you just as much! Service fills you with compassion. It also gives you a heart

> *The service you render to others will benefit them. But it will help you just as much!*

of gratitude, and the confidence that comes from obedience. Serving others is something God expects of us. When we do it obediently, He shapes us into men and servant leaders He can use more and more to show people everywhere how much He loves them.

"Whatever you do, whether in word or deed, do it all in the name of the Lord Jesus."

Colossians 3:17

Experiencing
Total
Growth

Spiritual Growth: How God Builds a Man

Being in Royal Rangers is about becoming the best version of you possible. You were born a male, so God wants you to become an extraordinary man!

In building men, God has never deviated from His pattern. He has always built men by starting them out as boys. Not even when He sent His own Son, Jesus, did He change His plan. Jesus started as a baby who was born in a poor family, raised in a small town with His mom and stepdad, who was a carpenter. Jesus developed physically like every other boy and young man.

So, God always builds men from the same starting point. Guys love it when we start showing signs that we are becoming men—deeper voice, stronger muscles, facial hair, etc.

Obviously, most of these signs are outward, or physical, and will naturally happen with a healthy diet, exercise, and sleep. However, the inside stuff that makes a man a man is not so automatic. It will only develop in you if you put effort into it. The danger is when you let yourself become distracted by the natural and progressive development of the outside stuff but fail to invest yourself in the less obvious but far more important inside stuff.

> *Only by assuming personal responsibility for the inside stuff will you mature into an exceptional man.*

Your dad and mom, your pastors, your Rangers leaders, and other godly influences can encourage you to develop the inside stuff, but they can't do it for you. It is your responsibility. Only by assuming personal responsibility for the inside stuff will you mature into an exceptional man. Everything you do in Royal Rangers is intended to help you in this exciting journey.

God designed boys and young men everywhere to want three things—and He uses these to make us exceptional men if we will let Him—*adventurous* fun, strength of *character*, and a deeply personal *task*, or purpose, to live for. And He uses these to build boys and young men so they get their *ACT* together and become real men.

God Builds Men with *Adventure*: Following Jesus Is Never Boring!

When God builds men, He starts with *adventure*. Like to hike, hunt, or fish? Play ball or watch sports? Listen to or play your music? Take photos, edit videos, or produce podcasts? Build or fix things? Help people by mowing the yard of a neighbor who's sick or in need? These are fun things guys like to do. We dream of adventure—going places, testing our limits, doing things that matter, and having fun! Do you realize God made you to enjoy adventure? He did! The Bible says God rides His chariot on the thunder. Sounds like fun, doesn't it? God has fun, and so can you.

The greatest adventure God gives you is life itself, but we should never attempt life on our own. God asks you to go on an adventure with Him. To do that requires faith or trust in God. Trust that God will never let you down, leave you behind, or forget about you. That sounds risky, doesn't it? But that is the very nature of adventure. It is characterized by a measure of the unseen or the unknown. That is exactly what makes adventure so fun, and without adventure, your Christian life will be boring. The cure is adventure!

When God asks you to follow Him, it will be an adventure for sure! He will ask you to do things that will require you to trust Him. If you take on His adventure, it will far surpass any adventure you could create for yourself. Only when you take on His adventures will you truly become a man who gets to know God in a personal and close way. Until you adventure with Him, God will be a distant, impersonal, and faceless figure. However, when you trust Him and adventure with Him, you will really know Him.

Adventuring with God involves loving Him and loving others as much as you love yourself. Wow! Sounds wild, doesn't it? It really is. Jesus said the Greatest Commandment is to love God with all your heart, soul, and mind. The next most important is to love others just like you love yourself (Matthew 22:37–39). Take note of this!

Adventuring with God is not optional. It is a command. Adventure is part of the way God builds a man. No adventure? No journey to manhood! No adventure with God, then your Christian life will be boring!

Real men have learned to risk it all to adventure with God. They learn to love Him with everything they have and to love others as much as they love themselves. Young men who play it safe slowly and naturally become men physically on the outside but remain immature kids on the inside. God transforms boys into men on adventures! It's pure adrenaline, on-your-feet-learning with God. It's never boring and always exciting. But neither is it optional because loving God and loving people is required for real adventure. So trust God and follow Him. You won't be disappointed!

What kind of adventures do you expect God might lead you into? Start a business? Play a sport? Marry or remain single? Become a missionary, pastor, or evangelist? Speak to a classmate about Jesus? Whatever it is, you can be sure it will be exciting and will shape you into a godly man!

God Forges Men's *Character*: Your Inside Stuff Is What Makes You Strong!

Besides adventure, God adds *character* as He builds a man. Character is our inside strength that comes in the form of brainpower, creative talents and abilities, emotional stability, moral and spiritual strength, and more. Is the character strength God gives you to show off or to take advantage of people? Of course not! It is to serve others, defend the defenseless, and to protect the ones we love.

Have you ever realized it is easier to pull people down and hold them there than it is to lift them up? It takes real strength and courage to lift people, and only the weight of unkind actions, words, and attitudes to hold them down. Guys who live as lids, who hold others back, are weak inside. However, guys who have character and who lift others are truly strong. It takes character to be a real man who cares about and builds up his inner strength.

Growing strong on the inside is not something we can do well on our own. We have to rely on the Holy Spirit to shape us from the inside out. The real you is the inside you. When you ask Jesus to come into your heart, to forgive your sins, and to be your Friend and the Leader of your life, His Spirit lives inside you. Then, if you let Him, the Holy Spirit will work on you and shape you to be more and more like Jesus. How awesome is that? Being made strong and powerful like Jesus!

The Holy Spirit will make you strong on the inside. This is the "Great Empowerment"—the Holy Spirit gives you power for life and ministry, builds your character, and focuses your God-given abilities. The inside stuff is what makes you truly strong. The Holy Spirit has unlimited strength, and He wants to share it all *with you* if you will let Him.

God Reveals a Personal *Task* for Each Man: You Have a Divine Purpose!

Finally, God builds into men a drive to accomplish a special *task*. This gives you direction and purpose. Adventure and strength focused on a special task makes you a real man!

Men who love adventure only for the sake of fun and who use their strength just to show off are guys who wreck themselves. Take, for example, Samson the Old Testament leader who before asking God to forgive him, landed himself in a work prison, weakened, with his eyes gouged out. God had given him a love for *adventure* and challenge plus great physical strength. Samson was taught by his parents to develop his moral *character* for the *task* of delivering his nation from the grip of their oppressors. But instead, he played games with God, preferring to create his own adventure (rather than trusting God to lead him on a truly great adventure). Samson used his strength for selfish gain rather than to accomplish his special task of serving others.

Your pastors and Royal Rangers leaders are excellent examples of the kind of men you can copy. They love adventure, they are morally and spiritually strong, and they are focused on serving their family, the church, and *you*! They focus their *adventure* and *character* strength on a special *task*, or purpose—being God's allies to tell the whole world about His love. We call this the Great Commission, the awesome task of showing everyone in the whole world God's amazing love! God will show you your special role in this task as you obediently go on an *adventure* with Him.

Now that you know how God builds a man, are you willing to go on an *adventure* with Him? Are you willing to let the Holy Spirit shape your *character*? Are you willing to assume your special *task* in life? Get your *ACT* together, become a man! Let God build your life. If you do, it will be full of *adventure*, strong *character*, and a special *task*. That is what being a Royal Ranger is all about—becoming the best version of you, the best man you can be. You were born a male, so let God shape you into the extraordinary man He wants you to become!

A Guy's Journey to Manhood

Young men need a vision of godly manhood. This book is every guy's guide on the journey. It is recommended for Discovery, Adventure, and Expedition Rangers, as well as adult leaders.

Order at RoyalRangers.com (item 02-0618).

Physical Growth: How God Builds a Temple

Physical growth is signified by one of the four gold points of the Royal Rangers Emblem. The gold points are the easiest for others to see. You grow mentally, socially, and spiritually. And you are growing day-by-day into the physical form of a man. In some ways, that growth may seem to occur quickly. In other ways, it may seem slow.

Some of your friends may seem to be growing faster than you. They're growing taller and stronger. But you may feel like you're not growing at all. Guys don't grow at the same speed. You may not like the speed you're growing at, but there's not much you can do about it. The main thing, however, is to make sure your body has what it needs to grow into a strong, healthy adult.

Building Blocks for Good Physical Health

Anytime a builder starts a new house, he begins with a strong foundation. The foundation is the part of the house that rests on the ground. It supports the rest of the house. A strong foundation is one key part of building a house that will last a long time and keep you safe in all kinds of weather.

Your body is like a house. It's the package within which your spirit lives and experiences life. In fact, the Bible teaches that a Christian's body is a temple of the Holy Spirit (1 Corinthians 6:19). When we invite Christ into our life, His Spirit comes to live inside us. And you know how it is when you have a guest to your home, right? You tidy up, of course! You should take good care of your body because you have the Holy Spirit living in you full-time. He's not just a guest; He is our Friend, our Confidant, and our Guide.

What's more, it's though your body that you grasp the concepts of sight, smell, taste, sound, and touch. Much of what you are able to do will be directly related to the strength, health, and condition of your body. That's why it's vital to keep your body in good shape. If you take good care of your body, it will serve you well for years.

Four Habits of Healthy Living

These four habits will give you a strong base for health and fitness. If you regularly apply these, you'll have a strong healthy body. Such a body will let you enjoy new things as you live.

> "For we know that if the earthly tent we live in is destroyed, we have a building from God, an eternal house in heaven, not built by human hands"
>
> (2 Corinthians 5:1).

Eat Right

Eating a good diet is crucial to your physical growth. As your body grows into adulthood, it needs a regular supply of nutrients. The United States Department of Agriculture (USDA) suggests these guidelines to help you pick the best food and know how much to eat.

Balancing Calories

- Enjoy your food, but eat less.
- Avoid oversized portions.

Foods to Increase

- Make half your plate fruits and vegetables.
- Make at least half your grains whole grains.
- Switch to fat-free or low-fat (1%) milk.

Foods to Reduce

- Don't eat too much salt. Compare sodium in foods like soup, bread, and frozen meals and choose the foods with lower numbers.
- Drink water instead of sugary drinks.

More information on selecting the right foods for a healthy, balanced diet can be found at ChooseMyPlate.gov.

Play Hard

Exercise plays a big role in being strong and healthy. It can help you feel better. It can help you have more energy. And it can also improve your mood. Experts suggest that guys your age get an hour or more of moderate to vigorous physical activity every day.

Exercise has some very important benefits:

- **Exercise benefits your body and your mind.** Exercise helps keep muscles working properly. It also causes the body to make something called endorphins. These endorphins can help you feel happier.

- **Exercising can help you get in shape.** Exercise burns calories. It keeps your muscles in good shape and it helps you stay at a healthy weight.

- **Exercise helps cut the risk of some diseases.** Being a healthy weight cuts your risk of type 2 diabetes and high blood pressure. These diseases are becoming more common in kids and teens.

Exercise can take many different forms. Any activity that gets your muscles working can be a great way to promote your physical growth.

Rest Well

Everybody needs rest. You can only operate for so long until you begin to shut down because of lack of rest. Just like eating, sleep is required for you to grow and be healthy.

Sleep lets your body rest and refresh. It lets your brain reset and prepares you for another day. Scientists think sleep is when your brain archives information and solves problems.

Guys your age typically need about nine to eleven hours of sleep each night. How much sleep you need can be judged by how you feel. When people don't get enough sleep, they are cranky or clumsy. They have problems concentrating. And they have trouble staying awake. If you regularly seem to have these issues, you may not be getting enough sleep. Go to bed earlier and see if it helps. Getting rid of your symptoms could be that simple.

There's more to resting well than just getting enough sleep. Sometimes, you can rest by just changing activities. Reading a book, drawing a picture, listening to music, or working on a hobby can be good ways to enjoy some time away from normal activities.

Whatever form of rest you take, be sure to listen to your body and mind. Find a form of rest that helps you recharge for the next round of activity.

Stay Clean

Keeping your body clean is important. Everyone needs to practice good personal cleanliness. It can be particularly valuable for guys your age. Your body soon will be going through a stage known as puberty. When that happens, some important changes will take place. Your voice will begin to deepen. You may grow more body hair and your muscles may get larger and stronger for no apparent reason. These are normal and natural changes. They are a typical part of a guy's development.

These changes are related to a number of new chemicals called hormones your body develops at this stage. These hormones can cause some unpleasant changes, too. There may be an increase in body odor from sweat. Or you may have a skin problem like acne. Or, you may have both. These problems can be usually managed by using good hygiene habits.

DEODORANT

- **Body odor:** Most people deal with body odor by using deodorant and antiperspirant after showering. A deodorant is a product typically made as a spray, a solid stick, or a gel. You can apply it to the parts of your body that produce the most sweat and odor, your armpits. Deodorants help kill bacteria that causes odor. Antiperspirants are used in the same way but work differently. They keep you from sweating. Deodorants and antiperspirants are often found together in one product.

- **Skin care:** Another common by-product of your physical development is an increase in the body oils on your skin. These oils can clog the pores of your skin and cause acne. Acne is small red blemishes. Acne can often be prevented or controlled by washing your skin regularly. It also helps to avoid food or drinks that contain large amounts of sugar or oil. Chocolate, soda pop, and potato chips are examples of things with lots of sugar and oil. Special soaps can also help you treat acne. Your doctor can prescribe medication if you need it.

- **Hair:** Keeping your hair clean can be a major factor in presenting a clean image. You should wash your hair every day if possible. Keep it looking neat by combing or brushing it before it dries. If your hair tends to be dry or uncontrollable use a conditioner. Conditioner adds moisture and nutrients to your hair.

• **Teeth:** Your teeth should be brushed at least twice daily. It's good to brush after every meal and at bedtime. Brushing your teeth reduces the likelihood of tooth decay and gum disease. This helps to ensure your teeth serve you well throughout life. Brushing also helps rid your mouth of bacteria that cause bad breath.

Alcohol, Tobacco, and Other Harmful Drugs

Almost everyone knows that smoking causes cancer, emphysema, and heart disease. It can shorten your life by ten years or more. A smoker can spend thousands of dollars a year on his addiction. So why are people still smoking?

The answer is addiction. Tobacco contains nicotine, a highly addictive drug. Like heroin or other addictive drugs, the body and mind quickly become dependent on the nicotine in cigarettes, chewing tobacco, cigars, etc.

Alcohol is likewise a very hazardous drug. In some forms, alcohol can be a very useful product. It can be used as a cleaner or to kill germs. When a person drinks alcohol, it gets into his bloodstream. Then, it affects the central nervous system. The brain and spinal cord are part of the central nervous system. The central nervous system controls virtually all body functions. Alcohol acts as a depressant. That means it slows the function of nearly every part of the body. It alters the way a person thinks. It alters the emotions. Alcohol also alters vision, hearing, and even movement.

If you've never tried using any of these drugs—YOU'RE SMART, DON'T START. If you have tried them, STOP NOW! The longer you use drugs the more addicted you become. If you need help, talk to your pastor. You can also talk to your Royal Rangers leader or school counselor. Look for help online. Many Web sites provide valuable information about overcoming addictions. But don't be afraid to ask for help. There are many ministries and programs available to help. You've got a lot of people on your side.

Health and Fitness Is a Lifestyle

Healthy physical development requires a lifestyle that includes all the building blocks of good health and fitness. It requires more than exercising once in a while. It requires more than going on a short-term diet. It's about making a choice, setting a goal, and sticking with it.

"Don't you know that you yourselves are God's temple and that God's Spirit dwells in your midst? If anyone destroys God's temple, God will destroy that person; for God's temple is sacred, and you together are that temple"
(1 Corinthians 3:16,17).

Partner with friends who practice good health habits. Encourage each other to stay fit. Encourage friends and family members to practice good health habits, too. Praise their progress along the way. Take pride in your physical condition. You'll be amazed at how much better you'll feel about yourself in every way. Take care of your body, and it will take care of you!

Eat Right
Play Hard
Rest Well
Stay Clean

Continuing the Process: Looking Ahead to Adventure Rangers

As your time in Discovery Rangers draws to a close, you will no doubt look back and recount lots of great experiences. Each one has been a step along the path of growing into the man God created you to be—mentally, physically, spiritually, and socially.

But your path of growth and achievement doesn't end with Discovery Rangers. It's just prepared you for the next step, moving on to Adventure Rangers.

Adventure Rangers is for middle school guys. It's structured in much the same way as the other Royal Rangers groups but features some important differences making it more suitable for middle school guys—the challenges are bigger and the opportunities are greater. So get ready for an *adventure*! Your time in Adventure Rangers has the potential of being your best, most-exciting days in Royal Rangers.

Frontiersmen Camping Fellowship

Frontiersmen Camping Fellowship (FCF) is a special program of Royal Rangers that promotes fellowship, personal development, Christian service, and a greater commitment to the ideals and principles of the Royal Rangers ministry while utilizing the symbols and imagery of the early American frontiersman.

FCF provides young men an excellent way to continue growing in Royal Rangers while reaching out to serve others at the same time.

Information on the membership requirements for FCF can be found in the *Frontiersmen Camping Fellowship Handbook* (item 02-0540) or online at Royal Rangers.com.

Here are some great goals to shoot for in Adventure Rangers:

- Earn your Adventure Gold award in Adventure or Expedition Rangers.
- If you have not already done so, earn your Discovery Rangers Gold Eagle award before graduating from Adventure Rangers.

www.RoyalRangers.com

Appendix A
DISCOVERY RANGERS
ADVANCEMENT
LOGBOOK

New Member Requirements

As a new Discovery Ranger, the following requirements must be met before you can earn your first
advancement step (the White Falcon award):

	Date Complete	Leader's Initials

○ Be a boy in the third, fourth, or fifth grade.

○ Complete your outpost's requirements
for new members, if any.

○ Recite from memory each of the following:
- Royal Rangers Pledge
- Royal Rangers Code
- Royal Rangers Motto
- Meaning of the points of the
  Royal Rangers Emblem
- Golden Rule

○ Read the booklet *Preventing Child and Substance
Abuse* and talk about what you have read with
your parents or legal guardians. This booklet can
be found online at RoyalRangers.com.

○ Attend three regular Discovery
Rangers meetings.
Dates attended: _____ _____ _____

Awarded New Member Status:

Year 1 - Trail to the GOLD FALCON

After completing the new member requirements, you can begin working towards earning the first year medal in Discovery Rangers—the Gold Falcon award. The Trail to the Gold Falcon consists of five steps. As you complete each step, you are eligible to receive the corresponding award.

	Date Complete	Leader's Initials
WHITE FALCON		
Earn 1 orange Bible merit ☑ _____	_____	_____
Earn 1 blue or green skill merit ☑ _____	_____	_____
Completed White Falcon award:	_____	_____
RED FALCON		
Earn 1 additional orange Bible merit ☑ _____	_____	_____
Earn 1 additional blue or green skill merit ☑ _____	_____	_____
Completed Red Falcon award:	_____	_____
BRONZE FALCON		
Earn 1 additional orange Bible merit ☑ _____	_____	_____
Earn 1 additional blue or green skill merit ☑ _____	_____	_____
Completed Bronze Falcon award:	_____	_____

	Date Complete	Leader's Initials

SILVER FALCON

Earn 1 additional orange Bible merit
☑ _____

Earn 1 additional blue or green skill merit
☑ _____

Earn 1 of the required blue skill merits*
☐ Bible Knowledge
☐ Global Missions
☐ First Aid Skills

Earn 1 red or gold leadership merit
☑ _____

Completed Silver Falcon award:

GOLD FALCON

○ Recite again from memory each of
the following. This is in addition to
the recitation for the new member
requirements.

- Royal Rangers Pledge
- Royal Rangers Code
- Royal Rangers Motto
- Meaning of the points of the Royal
Rangers Emblem
- Golden Rule

Completed Gold Falcon award:

*The required blue skill merit can be completed
at any time in Year 1. It must be earned before
you can receive the Gold Falcon award.

Year 2 - Trail to the GOLD HAWK

Once you have earned the Gold Falcon award, you can continue your progress along the Discovery Rangers Advancement Trail by pursuing the Gold Hawk award.

	Date Complete	Leader's Initials

WHITE HAWK

Earn 1 additional orange Bible merit
☑ _____

Earn 1 additional blue or green skill merit
☑ _____

    Completed White Hawk award:

RED HAWK

Earn 1 additional orange Bible merit
☑ _____

Earn 1 additional blue or green skill merit
☑ _____

    Completed Red Hawk award:

BRONZE HAWK

Earn 1 additional orange Bible merit
☑ _____

Earn 1 additional blue or green skill merit
☑ _____

    Completed Bronze Hawk award:

SILVER HAWK

Earn 1 additional orange Bible merit
☑ _____

Earn 1 additional blue or green skill merit
☑ _____

Earn 1 additional of the required
blue skill merits*
    ☐ Bible Knowledge
    ☐ Global Missions
    ☐ First Aid Skills

	Date Complete	Leader's Initials

Earn 1 additional red or
gold leadership merit

☑ _____

Completed Silver Hawk award: _____ _____

GOLD HAWK

○ Recite again from memory each of the
following. This is in addition to the recitation for the Gold Falcon award.

- Royal Rangers Pledge _____ _____
- Royal Rangers Code _____ _____
- Royal Rangers Motto _____ _____
- Meaning of the points of the Royal
  Rangers Emblem _____ _____
- Golden Rule _____ _____

○ Be a Gold Falcon award recipient at
least six months or be a graduate of
third grade. _____ _____

○ Serve in one or more leadership positions in Discovery Rangers for at least
six months. _____ _____

○ Show your ability to present the plan
of salvation to someone. _____ _____

Completed Gold Hawk award: _____ _____

*The second required blue skill merit can
be completed at any time in Year 2. It must
be earned before you can receive the
Gold Hawk award.

Year 3 - Trail to the GOLD EAGLE

Now that you've earned the Gold Hawk award, you can begin the final part of your Discovery Rangers Advancement Trail—the Trail to the Gold Eagle. Keep working and don't give up! You're almost there!

WHITE EAGLE

	Date Complete	Leader's Initials
Earn 1 additional orange Bible merit ☑ _____	_____	_____
Earn 1 additional blue or green skill merit ☑ _____	_____	_____
Completed White Eagle award:	_____	_____

RED EAGLE

Earn 1 additional orange Bible merit ☑ _____	_____	_____
Earn 1 additional blue or green skill merit ☑ _____	_____	_____
Completed Red Eagle award:	_____	_____

BRONZE EAGLE

Earn 1 additional orange Bible merit ☑ _____	_____	_____
Earn 1 additional blue or green skill merit ☑ _____	_____	_____
Completed Bronze Eagle award:	_____	_____

SILVER EAGLE

Earn 1 additional orange Bible merit
☑ _____   _____ _____

Earn 1 additional of the required
blue skill merits*
    ☐ Bible Knowledge
    ☐ Global Missions   _____ _____
    ☐ First Aid Skills

	Date Complete	Leader's Initials
Earn 2 additional red or gold leadership merits		
☑ _____	_____	_____
☑ _____	_____	_____
Completed Silver Eagle award:	_____	_____

GOLD EAGLE

○ Recite again from memory each of
the following. This is in addition to the
recitation for the Gold Hawk award:

- Royal Rangers Pledge   _____ _____
- Royal Rangers Code   _____ _____
- Royal Rangers Motto   _____ _____
- Meaning of the points of the Royal
  Rangers Emblem   _____ _____
- Golden Rule   _____ _____

○ Be a Gold Hawk award recipient at
least nine months or be a graduate of
fourth grade.   _____ _____

○ Serve in one or more leadership positions in Discovery Rangers for an additional six months, for a total of twelve
months.   _____ _____

○ Show your ability to present the plan
of salvation to someone.   _____ _____

Completed Gold Eagle award: _____ _____

*The third required blue skill merit can be com-
pleted at any time in Year 3. It must be earned
before you can receive the Gold Eagle award.

Bronze Buffalo Awards

When you have earned the Gold Eagle award, you can earn Bronze Buffalo awards. The award insignia is a bronze buffalo pin worn on the cloth portion of your Gold Eagle award medal. A bronze star insignia can also be worn on the Gold Eagle award ribbon. You may earn and wear up to two Bronze Buffaloes.

	Date Complete	Leader's Initials
BRONZE BUFFALO 1		
Earn 1 additional orange Bible merit		
☑ _____	_____	_____
Earn 2 additional blue or green skill merits		
☑ _____	_____	_____
☑ _____	_____	_____
Earn 1 additional red or gold leadership merit		
☑ _____	_____	_____
Completed Bronze Buffalo 1:	_____	_____
BRONZE BUFFALO 2		
Earn 1 additional orange Bible merit		
☑ _____	_____	_____
Earn 2 additional blue or green skill merits		
☑ _____	_____	_____
☑ _____	_____	_____
Earn 1 additional red or gold leadership merit		
☑ _____	_____	_____
Completed Bronze Buffalo 2:	_____	_____

Merit Completion Checklist

There are currently over 200 skill merits available to earn in Royal Rangers, and new merits are added regularly. RoyalRangers.com contains a list of all the merits currently available as well as requirements for each merit.

Note: Although you may earn merits from any color category, not all merits may be used to satisfy advancement requirements in Discovery Rangers. Refer to the preceding pages for details.

Blue Merits

	Date Complete	Leader's Initials		Date Complete	Leader's Initials
Art	___	___	In-line Skating	___	___
Astronomy	___	___	Insect Study	___	___
Basic Sign Language	___	___	Junior Bible Quiz	___	___
Basketry	___	___	Lashing	___	___
BB Gun	___	___	Law Enforcement	___	___
BGMC	___	___	Marksmanship	___	___
Bible Knowledge*	___	___	Models & Designs	___	___
Bible Reading	___	___	Music	___	___
Bird Study	___	___	National Prayer Center	___	___
Chess	___	___	Painting	___	___
Church	___	___	Pets	___	___
Coin Collecting	___	___	Pioneer Lore	___	___
Collections	___	___	Presidents	___	___
Compass	___	___	Railroading	___	___
Cooking	___	___	Reading	___	___
Darts	___	___	Rocketry	___	___
Disability Awareness	___	___	Roller Skating	___	___
Dog Care	___	___	Rope Craft	___	___
Family Life	___	___	Rowing	___	___
Fingerprinting	___	___	Safety	___	___
Fire Craft	___	___	Sculpture	___	___
Firearm Safety	___	___	Senior Citizens	___	___
First Aid Skills*	___	___	Space Exploration	___	___
Fishing	___	___	Tool Craft	___	___
Global Missions*	___	___	Weather	___	___
Hobby	___	___	Wildlife	___	___
Ice Skating	___	___			

*Required blue skill merit

Green Merits

	Date Complete	Leader's Initials		Date Complete	Leader's Initials
Academics	___	___	First Aid-CPR	___	___
Adv. Disability Awareness	___	___	Football	___	___
Advanced Marksmanship	___	___	Forestry	___	___
Advanced Swimming	___	___	Gardening	___	___
Air Rifle	___	___	Global Missions*	___	___
Amateur Radio	___	___	Healthy Body*	___	___
American History	___	___	Highlands	___	___
Archery	___	___	Hiking	___	___
Aviation	___	___	Home Repair	___	___
Bachelor	___	___	Home Safety	___	___
Backpacking	___	___	Horsemanship	___	___
Baseball	___	___	Indian Lore	___	___
Basketball	___	___	International Service	___	___
BB Gun	___	___	Knife and Hawk	___	___
Bible Knowledge*	___	___	Leather Craft	___	___
Bible Quiz	___	___	Nature Study	___	___
Bible Reading	___	___	Orienteering	___	___
Bugling	___	___	Photography	___	___
Camp Safety	___	___	Pioneering	___	___
Camping	___	___	Plant Science	___	___
Canoeing	___	___	Pottery	___	___
Carpentry	___	___	Primitive Shelters	___	___
Christian Missions	___	___	Primitive Snares	___	___
Christian Service	___	___	Public Speaking	___	___
Church History	___	___	Puppeteer	___	___
Communications	___	___	Reptile Study	___	___
Computers	___	___	Salesmanship	___	___
Convoy of Hope	___	___	Skateboarding	___	___
Crime Prevention	___	___	Soccer	___	___
Cycling	___	___	Sports	___	___
Dutch Oven Cooking	___	___	Stamp Collecting	___	___
Emergency Preparedness	___	___	Swimming	___	___
Energy	___	___	Tennis	___	___
Environmental Science	___	___	Truck Transportation	___	___
Family History	___	___	Wood Carving	___	___
Fire Safety	___	___	Wrestling	___	___

*Required green skill merit

Silver Merits

	Date Complete	Leader's Initials		Date Complete	Leader's Initials
Advanced Archery	___	___	Masonry	___	___
Advanced Backpacking	___	___	Medicine	___	___
Air Rifle	___	___	Metalwork	___	___
American Cultures	___	___	Model Rocketry	___	___
Animal Husbandry	___	___	Motor Boating	___	___
Architecture	___	___	Mountain Biking	___	___
Atomic Energy	___	___	Oceanography	___	___
Auto Mechanics	___	___	Pageantry	___	___
Bible Doctrines*	___	___	Paintball	___	___
Bible Reading	___	___	Plumbing	___	___
Black Powder	___	___	Public Health	___	___
Black Powder Shooting	___	___	Rappelling	___	___
Boating	___	___	Rock Climbing	___	___
Budget & Finance*	___	___	Sailing	___	___
Chemistry	___	___	Scholarship	___	___
Cinematography	___	___	Scuba Diving	___	___
Citizenship*	___	___	Shotgun Safety	___	___
Dentistry	___	___	Shotgun Shooting	___	___
Drafting	___	___	Sign Language	___	___
Economics	___	___	Skiing	___	___
Electricity	___	___	Skin Diving	___	___
Electronics	___	___	Small Bore Safety	___	___
Engineering	___	___	Small Bore Shooting	___	___
Farm & Ranch Mgmt	___	___	Snowboarding	___	___
Farm Mechanics	___	___	Soil & Water Conservation	___	___
Fine Arts Festival	___	___	Solar Science	___	___
Fly Fishing	___	___	Speed the Light	___	___
Foreign Language	___	___	Surveying	___	___
Geology	___	___	Track	___	___
Golf	___	___	Traffic Safety	___	___
Graphic Arts	___	___	Veterinary Medicine	___	___
Hide Tanning	___	___	Water Safety Instructor	___	___
Home Miss. – Construction	___	___	Water Skiing	___	___
Hunter Education/Safety	___	___	Whitewater Rafting	___	___
Journalism	___	___	Wilderness Survival	___	___
Kayaking	___	___	Winter Camping	___	___
Landscape Architecture	___	___	Woodworking	___	___
Law	___	___	World Missions	___	___
Lifesaving	___	___	World Miss. - Construction	___	___
Mammals	___	___	Youth Missions (AIM)	___	___

*Required silver skill merit

Orange Bible Merits

	Date Complete	Leader's Initials		Date Complete	Leader's Initials
1 Chronicles	___	___	Genesis	___	___
1 Kings	___	___	Joel	___	___
1 Samuel	___	___	John	___	___
2 Chronicles	___	___	Jonah	___	___
2 Kings	___	___	Joshua	___	___
2 Samuel	___	___	Judges	___	___
Acts	___	___	Luke	___	___
Daniel	___	___	Mark	___	___
Deuteronomy	___	___	Matthew	___	___
Esther	___	___	Nehemiah	___	___
Exodus	___	___	Numbers	___	___
Ezra	___	___	Ruth	___	___

Bible 1-5

Red Leadership Merits

	Date Complete	Leader's Initials		Date Complete	Leader's Initials
Leadership 101	___	___	Leadership 104	___	___
Leadership 102	___	___	Leadership 105	___	___
Leadership 103	___	___	Leadership 106	___	___

Special Awards

	Date Complete	Leader's Initials		Date Complete	Leader's Initials
Medal of Valor	___	___	25-Mile Award	___	___
Medal of Courage	___	___	50-Mile Award	___	___
National Medal of Merit	___	___	100-Mile Award	___	___
Nat'l Outstanding Service	___		Tool Craft Safety Card	___	___
Missions Project Award	___	___	Firearm Safety Card	___	___
District Medal of Merit	___	___			
District Outstanding Serv	___	___			

See chapter 9 for information on special awards.

Junior Leadership Development

For details on the junior leadership development
process refer to chapter 20.

	Date *Complete*	*Leader's* *Initials*

JUNIOR LEADERSHIP FOUNDATIONS

See page 138 for details _____ _____

RANGER TRAINING CAMP (RTC)

See page 139 for details _____ _____

Universal Patch and Pin Placement Guide for Royal Rangers Uniforms

The following patch and pin placement guidelines apply to all Royal Rangers uniforms utilizing insignia (boys and leaders). Some patches are standard, required items and must be worn on all uniform shirts while other patches are optional. Required patches are indicated below in red.

**Universal
Patch and Pin
Placement Guide
for Royal Rangers
Uniforms**

PATCH FORMAT (Utility Uniform only)

Right Sleeve

Geographic patch (formerly district strip), centered, ½ inch below shoulder seam (required).

Outpost numerals, centered, touching the bottom edge of the geographic patch OR the staff patch (required).

Advancement level patch (boys) or Rangers Ministry Academy training level patch (leaders), centered ½ inch below outpost numerals.

Note: National and regional organizational leaders may wear the national staff patch in place of a geographic patch and outpost numerals.

Right Pocket

Event patch (any Royal Rangers event), centered on pocket.

ABOVE RIGHT POCKET

Group name tag (boys) or Royal Rangers name tag (leaders), centered above and along the top edge of the pocket (required).

FCF or RRA membership patch centered ½ inch above name tag.

Left Pocket

Training patch, centered on pocket.

Left Sleeve

Royal Rangers Emblem patch, centered, ½ inch below shoulder seam (required).

Local office insignia, centered ½ inch below Royal Rangers Emblem.

PIN FORMAT (Utility and Dress Uniforms)

Right Sleeve

Geographic patch (formerly district strip), centered, ½ inch below shoulder seam (required).

Outpost numerals, centered, touching the bottom edge of the geographic patch or the staff patch (required).

Advancement level patch (boys) or Rangers Ministry Academy training level patch (leaders) centered, ½ inch below outpost numerals.

Note: *National and regional organizational leaders may wear the national staff patch in place of a geographic patch and outpost numerals.*

Right Pocket

Event patch (any Royal Rangers event), centered on pocket.

Personal name tag (leaders only) engraved plastic, ¾" x 3", navy blue with white lettering, 2 lines of text, name & position. Boys may wear a special recognition pin, such as Outpost Ranger of the Year, FCF Scout name tag, or NSSP Ambassador name tag.

ABOVE RIGHT POCKET

Group name tag (boys) or Royal Rangers name tag (leaders), centered above and along the top edge of the pocket (required).

FCF membership pins, centered above and along the top edge of the name tag OR FCF or RRA membership patch, centered ½ inch above name tag.

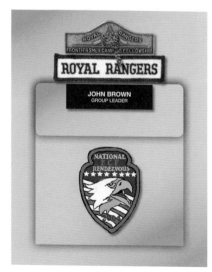

Left Pocket

Training patch, centered on pocket.

One medal, centered across the top edge of pocket. May not represent an award that is also represented by a ribbon above the pocket (not shown).

ABOVE LEFT POCKET

Ribbons, maximum of 18, centered above and along the top edge of the pocket. (Visit RoyalRangers.com for order of wear)

Royal Rangers International (RRI) support pin, RRA pin, centered, ½ inch above top row of ribbons.

Note: *Medals and ribbons may be worn at the same time, provided they do not represent the same awards.*

Left Sleeve

Royal Rangers Emblem patch, centered, ½ inch below shoulder seam (required).

Local office insignia centered, ½ inch below Royal Rangers Emblem.

DISCOVERY RANGERS VEST FRONT

Wearer's Right

Small Royal Rangers Emblem, centered, 3" down from top seam

Local office insignia, centered or evenly spaced, in one row, arranged in any order

Training patches, centered or evenly spaced, in one row, arranged in any order

Advancement patches arranged in straight rows and columns, in order as shown, edges touching, beginning at bottom inside edge of vest.

NOTE: Vertical and horizontal spacing may vary as needed on all items other than advancement patches, based on the size of the vest and number of items being displayed

Wearer's Left

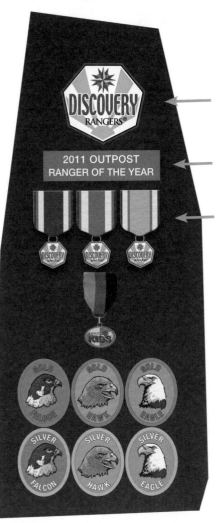

Group emblem, centered, 3" down from top seam

Special Recognition Pin (Outpost Ranger of the Year, etc.), centered

Award medals, maximum of six in two rows of three, centered or evenly spaced. Refer to national Royal Rangers Web site for order of wear.

Note: Medals earned in previous groups may be displayed on the awards vest, to the right of or below current medals (see order of wear).

NOTE: Vertical and horizontal spacing may vary as needed on all items other than advancement patches, based on the size of the vest and number of items being displayed

Universal
Patch and Pin
Placement Guide
for Royal Rangers
Uniforms

DISCOVERY RANGERS
VEST BACK

  Merit patches arranged neatly in
any order, beginning 2" below
collar, with sides touching →

 Activity patches (and Mile Award
patches) arranged in one or more
rows along the bottom edge, in
any order, with sides touching →

Index

A

Action Camps, 140

Advancement Trail, 52, 65–73

Advancement Logbook,
  See Appendix A

Adventure Rangers, 21, 63, 66, 72, 140, 169–171

Ambassadors in Mission, 145

Alcohol, 165, 166

Awards

  Index, 80

  Medal of Courage, 76, 80

  Medal of Merit

    District, 77, 80

    National, 76, 80

  Medal of Valor, 42, 76, 80

  Mile, 78, 80

  Missions Project, 77, 80, 145

  Outstanding Service

    District, 77, 80

    National, 77, 80

Awards vest, 78,
  See also Appendix B

B

Boys and Girls Missionary Challenge (BGMC), 145

C

Camporama, National, 43, 44, 63

Clean, 8, 9, 31, 163, 164

Code, Royal Rangers, 8, 9, 27–32

Convoy of Hope, 45, 145

D

Drugs, 165, 166

E

E3 Award, 72

Emblem, Royal Rangers, 8, 68, 69, 70, 104, 159

Events, District and National, 62, 63

Exercise, 24, 152, 162

Expedition Rangers, 21, 63, 72, 140

Experiences, the Seven, 18, 49–55

F

Fire Bible for Kids, 33

Firearm Safety Card, 79, 80

Flags

  Caring for, 39

  Displaying, 37, 38

Frontiersmen Camping Fellowship, 42, 63, 170

G

Gold Eagle award, 15, 19, 70, 71

Gold Falcon, 68

Gold Hawk, 69

Gold Medal of Achievement (GMA), 19, 42, 72, 73, 171

Gold Trail award 72, 73

Group Leadership Team, 95, 116, 119–122

Guy's Journey to Manhood, 157

Guy's Journey to Servant Leadership, 139

Index

H

Hear See Do Teach concept, 53, 83–85

History of Royal Rangers, 41–45

J

Junior Leadership Development, 137–140

Junior Leadership Foundations (JLF), 19, 54, 138

Junior Leadership Training Camps, 139

L

Leadership book, 139

Leadership positions, 103–116

Leadership Trail, 52

M

Manhood book, 157

Meetings, 120–122, 125–127, 134

MEGA Sports Camp, 145, 146

Membership, 68

Merit Camps, 139

Merits, 15–17, 66, 67

    Bible, 15, 16, 24, 66

    Leadership, 15, 16, 67, 138, 139

    Skill, 15, 16, 67

Motto, Royal Rangers, 8, 32, 104

N

New member, 68

P

PathFinder Missions, 145

Patrol of Excellence, 133–135

Patrol/Patrol System, 93–95, 97–101, 133

Physical growth, 159–163

Planning, 122, 129–131

Pledges

    Bible, 36

    Christian Flag, 36

    U.S. Flag, 36

    Royal Rangers, 36

R

Ranger Kids, 21, 71, 72, 73, 145

Recruit, *See* New member

Rendezvous, National FCF, 42, 63

S

Serve/Service, 55, 143–146

Service Trail, 52

SMART goals, 99, 100

Speed the Light, 145

T

Tobacco, 165

Tool Craft Safety Card, 79, 80

Trail of the Saber Award, 140

Training, *See* Junior Leadership Development

U

Uniforms, 54, 87–91, *See* also Appendix B